The
Holly Willoughby
Abduction Case

Katherine Smith

Contents

AUTHOR'S NOTE

The case of Gavin Plumb is somewhat unusual in that no physical crime took place. Plumb was convicted for what he was planning and talking about online rather than something he got around to actually doing. These sorts of cases are increasingly common today as justice systems and police forces adapt (as best they can) to the challenges and dangers posed by the internet. Once upon a time sex offenders would be isolated and adrift in society but these days they have their own online chat groups where they can hang out to share tales of their grubby deeds and perhaps even plot new crimes together. Efforts by law enforcement agencies to monitor these sorts of places and identify dangerous people are complex and difficult to say the least due to the vast size of the net. Many of the tech companies who facilitate these groups haven't always been a huge help either.

Gavin Plumb never met Holly Willoughby and never went anywhere near her house or the television studios where she worked for most of the week co-hosting This Morning. He never 'stalked' Holly Willoughby nor made any attempt to go to a place where he knew she would be. He did though spend the best part of two years in private chat groups talking (in graphic terms) about abducting her and the things he would do if she were his prisoner. He solicited (without any real sign of success) help in his attempt to put a kidnapping 'crew' together and purchased items (restraints, metal cable ties etc) that would potentially assist in an abduction.

The defence argued in court that Plumb's abduction plan was absurd and simply an online fantasy that he got carried away with due to the lonely emptiness of his life in the real world. Gavin Plumb and his defence team insisted that this was just a sick, horrible, and regrettable online fantasy that he never had any intention of doing for real and wouldn't have been capable of doing anyway. Gavin Plumb was a hugely overweight and patently unfit man who couldn't even drive. How was he supposed to kidnap Holly Willoughby?

The prosecution took a very different view on this strange and depressing case. They pointed out the dark criminal history of Gavin Plumb and the things he had done not in cyberspace but the real world. Plumb had two past criminal convictions for attempting to abduct and restrain four different women. This information certainly put a more complex (and damaging) gloss on the defence that his Holly Willoughby abduction talk was just that - merely talk. The more one learned about Gavin Plumb the more difficult it became to believe he was someone content to confine himself merely to vile online chat groups.

In the book that follows we will examine this bizarre and disturbing case in detail and try our best to make some sense of it if we can. Be warned that parts of this book unavoidably make for grim reading but there is no way to present a full picture of this case without all the details - however grim and unpleasant they might be. I sincerely hope too though that this book is respectful and sensitive in relation to Holly Willoughby and all the victims of Gavin Plumb - none of whom deserve to be connected to this awful man in any way. A list of selected references used in the research for this book can be found at the conclusion of the final chapter.

CHAPTER ONE

The Collector (which was a major influence on Stephen King's Misery) is a 1963 psychological novel by John Fowles. In the story (which is told from two perspectives), a man named Frederick Clegg collects butterflies and is completely detached from society and socially awkward and shy. Clegg, who inherited money from his parents and therefore doesn't need to go to work, purchases a remote cottage but when he ventures into town he becomes obsessed with a local art student named Miranda Grey. After secretly observing and spying on Miranda for a time, Clegg kidnaps her with the aid of chloroform and imprisons her in the cellar of his cottage - which he has carefully prepared for the latest addition to his 'collection'. Clegg promises not to harm or abuse Miranda and believes that if he can keep her there and shower her with gifts she will come to love him and agree to stay for good.

A battle of wills between these two very different people now unfolds. Clegg is a monster but a calm, delusional one who thinks that if he gives Miranda everything she requests in the form of books and art materials she will somehow come around and be happy to stay. He's always offended by the notion that he is a monster and constantly tries to reassure himself that he isn't doing anything strange or wrong. Frederick naively thinks he can create his own personal fantasy world with himself and Miranda together forever in the cottage. He learns though that in the real world you can't have everything you want or desire. Only in private fantasies and daydreams do you control the outcomes in life.

In the grim fantasy world of Gavin Plumb, his own version of Miranda Grey was the famous television presenter Holly Willoughby. Gavin Plumb was obsessed with a great many female celebrities (as his internet files testified) but Holly Willoughby was up there on a golden pedestal way beyond and above any of the others. He would refer to her simply as 'Holly' online as if she was the only person with that name in the entire world. Of course, most of the people he mixed with online knew exactly who he meant because the vast majority of his online activities, which once featured more healthy pursuits like football news and gaming, became ever more constrictive until they consisted almost entirely of private chat groups made up of men (many of whom were convicted sex offenders like Plumb) talking about all the horrible things they'd like to do to Holly Willoughby and other female presenters and celebrities.

These were bleak cyber dens of misogyny and violent sexual fantasies. Gavin Plumb was addicted to these awful online groups in the end. He would literally spend day and night there frantically messaging other members and posting endless pictures of Holly Willoughby. The ultimate fantasy of Gavin Plumb was to abduct Holly Willoughby and keep her captive as his own personal property to do with as he pleased. Plumb spent the best part of two years talking about this fantasy online. The basic fantasy was that he would abduct Holly Willoughby from her home and then keep her captive in an abandoned stable where she would be raped and abused. Plumb's fantasy stipulated that it would be impossible to return her without getting caught so at some point he would have to kill her.

In the end the fantasy got so elaborate and explicit it didn't sound like a fantasy at all. While the plan itself never made an awful lot of sense (Gavin Plumb was not famed for his high IQ), tedious logistics and mundane small details were interspliced with sexual fantasy. This made it feel suspiciously like an actual plan rather than mere fantasy - a fact which was not lost on the prosecution when this strange and depressing affair ended up in court. Gavin Plumb even seemed to start trying to recruit people online to help him abduct Holly Willoughby. He appeared to believe that the chat group he frequented was rife with professional criminals to whom abducting a celebrity would be no big deal at all.

However, unlike Frederick Clegg with Miranda Grey, Plumb never got as far as acting on his alleged kidnap plan. The plan never went beyond the confines of Plumb's computer and daydreams. In fact, Plumb insisted there was never a plan to begin with - at least not a real one. It was all make believe. It existed only in his head and in 'dark web' style private chatrooms, forums, and messages. Plumb insisted that all his talk of abducting Holly Willoughby was nothing more than sordid fan fiction. This was the defence that Gavin Plumb and his barrister would doggedly cling to right to the end when, much to his shock, he ended up in court for all the terrible things he had said and threatened to do on the internet.

Gavin Plumb desperately hoped the very idea of him - a portly out of shape man to say the least - undertaking some SAS style raid on Holly Willoughby's secure high walled CCTV and alarm festooned South West London home was so ludicrous that he couldn't possibly be found guilty. That hope quickly floated away in court when the prosecution barrister got her turn to question him and wasted no time in raking up his past convictions. A jury did not find the idea of him abducting Holly Willoughby ludicrous - especially when they were reminded of his criminal history and given stark evidence of Plumb's grim and vile online posts and video messages from the months before his arrest.

The master of Gavin Plumb's own downfall was none other than himself. Plumb had sowed the self-destructive seeds of his doom long before he landed in court on these bizarre planned kidnap and murder allegations. Not just through his obsessive and disturbing activity in the bleak corners of the internet where he endlessly discussed, in highly unpleasant (if somewhat unrealistic) detail, his plan to abduct Holly Willoughby but also his past conduct and convictions in the real world. Four women, two of them only sixteen at the time, were harrowing proof that Gavin Plumb was not merely an online fantasist. His past criminal convictions were not dark fan fiction or online fantasies. They really happened.

There were others too. An ex-partner who accused him of domestic violence and sexual abuse and an unnamed woman who said Plumb raped her in 2008. Gavin Plumb's history of violence and sexual abuse towards women - which resulted in two convictions and two prison sentences - afforded him few favours at his 2024 trial. Gavin Plumb's attempt in court to portray himself as an online fantasist who wasn't like that in real life was at odds with his ACTUAL history. This was a very obvious and serious handicap to Plumb's defence team in court. The best they could do was ask the jury not to hold past convictions from long ago against him and simply focus only on the case in hand. In the end that wasn't enough. It was impossible for the jury not to take Plumb's past convictions into consideration because they seemed very relevant to the charges he now faced.

And it wasn't a simple question of whether Gavin Plumb was capable of this audacious celebrity kidnapping himself (to which the answer would almost certainly be NO given that Plumb was obese, unfit, and didn't even drive or have a car). The question of whether Plumb had sought willing accomplices to aid him in this kidnapping was a considerable factor in the trial he would face in 2024. Plumb's electronic devices were chock full of evidence which proved beyond doubt he had solicited help online. There were thousands of private messages flying back and forth online where Plumb is plainly attempting to put a 'team' together for the purpose of abducting Holly Willoughby. There wasn't much proof though that anyone had actually agreed to help him.

Some of the men on these forums were patently disturbed but even they weren't crazy enough to commit themselves to helping someone they'd never met kidnap Holly Willoughby. They were not that stupid. They knew that Gavin Plumb's unrefined and plainly deficient plan of action only had one ending - abject failure leading to arrest and prison. Would though Gavin Plumb have at least tried to carry out the abduction if he had others stupid and crazy enough to help him? This was the question a jury would have to consider. It was the whole foundation of the case. When it came to Holly Willoughby, was Gavin Plumb simply an obsessed bedroom fantasist or was he a genuine threat? The prosecution case was that Plumb never saw himself as a 'lone wolf' in this abduction. They argued that Plumb saw himself as a ringleader. He knew he needed assistance and much of his online activity was geared to this end.

There was one other big difference between Gavin Plumb and Frederick Clegg. Plumb made no promises not to harm or abuse Holly Willoughby. In fact, the way Gavin Plumb told it online and in private messages, that was the whole point of the alleged kidnap plan in the first place. Disgusting cyber vomit on this theme poured from the dark corners of Plumb's mind to the dark corners of the net for the best part of two years. Though he would tell a courtroom he only thought about Holly Willoughby about five or six times a day, in reality Gavin Plumb had somehow turned typing all the horrible things he wanted to do to Willoughby into a full time job. Gavin Plumb's life was empty. He had no hobbies, no creative outlets, no group of friends. He lived alone. There were long periods when he couldn't even go outside due to his weight. Any employment was sporadic and usually short lived. Often left with literally nothing to do all day, Plumb, thanks to daytime television, began to develop an unhealthy obsession with Holly Willoughby. This obsession slowly but surely seemed to take over his entire life.

Gavin Plumb was born in Essex in February 1987. It was a typical working-class ordinary childhood of the type that millions have experienced. Gavin Plumb spent most of his life living in Harlow, Waltham Abbey and Loughton and has three brothers and a half-brother. His father was a man named Adrian Broad but Broad left the family when Gavin Plumb was very young - so young in fact that Gavin Plumb barely had any memories of him. Broad later said he didn't abandon the family and tried to stay in touch with his children. He said his contact being non-existent when his kids were very young was no fault of his own and then, when they got a bit older, they chose not to remain in contact with him. Gavin Plumb, despite being born Gavin Broad, therefore took the surname of his stepfather. Adrian Broad said the reason he lost contact with his kids when they were young is that he had nowhere to host them at weekends. Whatever the truth, he drifted out of their lives and didn't seem to be terribly missed.

Those that knew the young Gavin Plumb, who was raised by his mother (Mrs Plumb has studiously and sensibly kept out of the public eye and so very little is known about her) and stepfather (who worked as a security guard), described him as something of a mummy's boy. He could never do anything wrong as far as his mother was concerned - though Plumb would of course test this maternal loyalty in extreme ways. Nonetheless, it is said that his mother stood by him after his 2024 conviction and whenever he got into trouble in the past she always turned up in court. While she obviously didn't approve of his activities on the net and was disappointed by what she heard at Chelmsford Crown Court in 2024,, Plumb's mother most likely did not believe that her son ever intended to really kidnap and murder Holly Willoughby.

Mrs Plumb had known long before the events of 2023 and 2024 though that there was a darkness to her son. A troubled and unfathomable aspect to his character which had surfaced before. She must have hoped this side of him was long gone but in 2023 her son would land in his hottest water yet. No one could have possibly predicted though the odd and unusual circumstances of Plumb's latest brush with the law. Gavin Plumb was always big for his size but he didn't throw his weight around as a child or come off as a bully. Quite the opposite. He was actually, given his size, a strangely meek child - which was a contrast to his personality as an adult. The police later released the footage of Plumb's arrest in 2023 and Gavin Plumb comes off as a confident and assertive person in the footage. He isn't the least bit intimidated by his flat being full of police officers and even tells one of them off for smashing his door in. As a child and teenager though he was a less confident sort of character.

As an adult, Gavin Plumb DID exhibit cowardly bullying

tendencies but only with women. He never picked on anyone his own size. Plumb was about thirteen when his weight became a serious health problem and something he found impossible to get under control. He wasn't a very tall person either so the weight was even more of a burden. It would eventually get a lot worse too. Plumb would later become absolutely gargantuan in this thirties - to the point where he could barely stand up and suffered from constant pain. At that point he took drastic action and applied to have gastric band surgery. In a roundabout way this would actually become a subplot of his 2024 trial. The prosecution argued that Plumb's main motivation for losing weight had been so he was fit enough to participate in an abduction - with Holly Willoughby the designated target.

Gavin Plumb said his weight caused him great sadness when he was younger because he was too unfit to play football anymore. It made him feel estranged from normal boys his own age because they were all running around and full of energy whereas he was this unfit lumbering kid who just had to watch sadly from the side-lines rather than take part in anything. This was the story of his adult life too for the most part. Gavin Plumb came to feel that life was something which only happened to other people. It left him with deep and enduring feelings of bitterness and frustration. Gavin Plumb attended Burnt Mill School in Harlow, Essex. This school was established in 1962 and was a comprehensive when Plumb went there. The famous footballer (and later the England manager) Glenn Hoddle went to this school. These days the school is called Burnt Mill Academy.

Plumb, according to other ex-pupils, suffered from bullying at the school and was someone who stayed on the fringes of school life and kept himself to himself. He certainly wasn't confident or assertive in his early years. This detachment was a pattern that Plumb would later repeat for much of his adult life. In the last couple of places he lived before his 2023 arrest, most of his neighbours told the media that they never actually had a conversation with him and described Plumb as a reclusive sort of character. During his trial, Plumb told the court that he was not popular with girls at school and was - at best - always a friend and never a boyfriend. This is speculated to have left him with a lingering bitterness towards women - who he tended in the end to see as mere objects to be taken by force rather than human beings. His criminal convictions and later online activities revealed a disturbing misogynistic streak which seemed to have become increasingly dominant in his personality.

Gavin Plumb was not very academic at school and never terribly bright. When his online posts were later revealed in extensive detail they were, despite the fact they had been posted by someone in their mid to late thirties, riddled with childlike spelling mistakes. The best that Gavin Plumb could hope for when he left school was to follow in the footsteps of his stepfather and become a security guard. The defence tried to use the fact that Gavin Plumb was not the sharpest tool in the box to their advantage in the Holly Willoughby abduction trial. They argued that Plumb, besides the fact he was overweight and clumsy, lacked even a semblance of the intelligence and organisational planning required to successfully kidnap a major celebrity.

Gavin Plumb never had any great ambitions or much sense of direction in life. Because he had no goals and just ambled through a mundane low-wage/unemployment benefits sort of life with no connections or privilege to fall back on, Plumb became increasingly vulnerable to the rabbit hole of fantasy. Most of us prefer fantasy to harsh reality and Gavin Plumb was no different. The difference was the obnoxious and nasty brand of fantasy that appealed to him. He became addicted to sick online chat groups which were populated by sex offenders and stalkers. These were places where you could say anything you wanted. Plumb seemed to think that fantasy was a place you can permanently move into and stay - which it assuredly isn't. The tension between fantasy and reality became one of the salient factors in sealing the fate of Gavin Plumb. He began to rapidly lose his grip on the real world and that grip had never been very firm to begin with.

Although he was depicted in the media as some perpetual lifelong hermit loner who only ever existed online and rarely went outside (which did become the case for a time when his weight made it impossible for him to work or go outdoors), Gavin Plumb was the father of two children. This all happened when he was very young and ill equipped to cope with such responsibilities (although Gavin Plumb was probably never really equipped to be a supportive and dutiful parent at any time in his life). The mother of his children was a woman named Laura Roberts. Plumb had known Laura Roberts since they were eleven (they got to know each through Laura's sister being a classmate of Plumb) but they only started going out in their late teens.

It is safe to say that Laura Roberts did not exactly hit the jackpot with Gavin Plumb. Given a choice, he probably wouldn't have been the first person she chose to have children with. There is a photograph online of Plumb and Laura Roberts posing with their first child. Plumb is grinning like an idiot and seems genuinely happy. The smile of Laura Roberts for the benefit of the photograph is a trifle more forced and less natural. While it is impossible to look at this photograph now in a neutral way without using hindsight, there is something slightly off about Laura Roberts in the picture nonetheless. She looks more like someone is a hostage video than some happy young mother in love. Laura Roberts was petite and dark haired in the photograph. She was a fairly attractive young woman who looked like she could do a lot better than Gavin Plumb.

Laura had a son in 2007 and then fell pregnant again in 2008 with what turned out to be a daughter. Happy family life proved elusive though for Laura Roberts and Gavin Plumb. Though he later tried to blame Laura for things turning sour between them, it was in fact Gavin Plumb who caused all the problems. He was not cut out for family life and responsibilities - especially at such a young age. He was unreliable and often out of work. He was also abusive and controlling. Life with Gavin Plumb eventually turned into a nightmare for Laura Roberts. Laura later told the media, in the aftermath of his 2024 trial, that her life with Gavin Plumb had been awful and she was subject to a lot of violence in the few years they were together. She said she wasn't surprised at all to learn in 2023 that Gavin Plumb was planning to kidnap someone.

Laura wasn't surprised by news of Plumb's earlier convictions either. Laura Roberts said even if it hadn't been Holly Willoughby, Plumb would have been planning to kidnap someone else. She hated Gavin Plumb with a passion and let him have both barrels in the media when she finally got the chance to speak. Gavin Plumb briefly had a job at McDonald's around this time but he was often unemployed too. In the end there were arguments between Plumb and Laura and worse. He would beat and threaten her and she lived in constant fear. Gavin Plumb later said that Laura would tell him he was useless and make it plain he wasn't exactly her first choice when it came to a partner. He said this made life with Laura a misery for him. But life with Plumb was a much bigger misery for Laura.

Plumb didn't have to worry about domestic violence or being raped like Laura did with him. Laura Roberts was only 5 foot tall and tiny while Plumb was a huge hunk of a man. It was a complete mismatch. Laura said that Plumb became domineering and aggressive in the end. He often took all of her money and spent it on junk food. A friend of Laura Roberts told the media many years later (after the 2024 trial) that Gavin Plumb had seemed perfectly decent and normal at first but about eight months into his relationship with Laura (which lasted around three years in total) he turned violent and controlling and acted as if Laura was not a girlfriend or the mother of his children but some sort of mute slave who had to obey him at all times.

The horrified friend of Laura came to believe that Plumb was a disturbed and highly dangerous man who craved having a frightened woman under his complete control. Laura said that Gavin Plumb would even tightly control who she was allowed to talk to (thus estranging her from friends and family) so in the end she felt more like a lonely hostage or isolated prisoner than someone in a normal relationship. Laura believed that Gavin Plumb enjoyed it when she was scared of him. He enjoyed having that power over another person. At this early stage of his life we can already see then the signs of the dysfunction which would later land Gavin Plumb in prison on no less than three occasions. Gavin Plumb, predictably, told a very different story about his time with Laura Plumb when he spoke about his background in court. He described their relationship as toxic but pinned the blame on Laura and said she was the one who made it toxic by constantly belittling him and generally making his life a misery.

Gavin Plumb's attempt to put a more sympathetic spin on himself during his time with Laura Roberts was not terribly convincing. It was certainly a stretch to imagine that this huge and plainly dangerous man would ever willingly endure a situation where he was under the thumb and bullied by a tiny woman. While there was a brief period at the start where the couple seemed to get on and other periods where Laura seemed to stick it out purely for the sake of the children, it all quickly turned sour. It is hard to see really what Laura saw in Gavin Plumb (who was no Brad Pitt) in the first place. Perhaps she initially felt sorry for this apparently meek lonely teenage gentle giant and so developed a soft spot for him?

Despite the fact he was supposed to be with Laura Roberts (though the relationship was gradually crumbling) a woman named Ellie Hoad also dated Plumb for two months in 2007. Laura Roberts seemed to get the dark version of Plumb but Hoad got a more innocuous version. Ellie Hoad said Plumb was quiet, friendly and had a good sense of humour.

According to Ellie, although they went to the cinema a few times initially, Plumb spent most of his time playing video games and rarely if ever came outside - which perhaps explains why the relationship didn't last very long. A boyfriend who refuses to leave the house or go out is probably not the most interesting of companions in the long run.

Ellie Hoad said she was surprised when Gavin Plumb's crimes and Holly Willoughby abduction plan came to light in the media because she hadn't detected any darkness or malevolence about him. "I just can't get my head around it, that he's gone from the shy, quiet person I knew back all those years ago to now he wants to do this," she said.

As we have already noted, this was not the case for Laura Roberts though. She wasn't surprised at all when she learned about Plumb's convictions and crazy abduction scheme. Ellie Hoad knew Plumb for far less time than Laura Roberts and unlike Laura Roberts she didn't have to live with him. It seems likely that if she had lived with Plumb for an extended period then she might have seen the darkness and controlling nature of his character come out. Laura Roberts on the other hand knew Gavin Plumb long enough to know he was a dangerous man.

The police have since confirmed that Plumb was arrested for domestic violence while he was with Laura Roberts. This was the first inkling that Plumb was a dark character most likely destined to end up behind bars in the end. This prophecy came true much sooner than anyone, perhaps even Plumb himself, could have predicted. A lot of Gavin Plumb's tawdry fantasies at this time seemed to revolve around female air-stewardesses. These fantasies may have abounded from his day to day life in this specific period. Plumb had a job at the time servicing ticket machines in car parks and he often used the Stansted Express to get around to these car parks. The Stansted Express is a direct train service linking London Liverpool Street to London Stansted Airport. When he used the train, Plumb would quite often see female air-stewardesses on their way to work in their uniforms. This planted the seed of a truly insane plan in his mind. Plumb decided he would abduct one of these female air-stewardesses from the train.

CHAPTER TWO

In 2007, Gavin Plumb was handed a suspended sentence for the attempted kidnap of two air-stewardesses on the Stansted Express. Both of these incidents happened in August. He was only nineteen years old at the time. The second abduction attempt took place two days after the first one (the incidents were separate so Plumb did this not once but twice). These were truly bizarre crimes which caused the victims great fear and distress. Plumb used a fake imitation gun and threatening notes to try and force the victims off the train. In the note he handed to the victims, Plumb was threatening to shoot everyone on the train if they didn't do as he said. To say that Plumb was not thinking straight would be something of an understatement to say the least. Any vestige of logic, sanity or rational thinking had become a distant second to his all consuming desire to possess his very own air-stewardess. Trying to abduct someone on a train was plainly not an idea cooked up by a rocket scientist. There was little chance of this plan actually working.

Because he didn't have a car or drive, Plumb's plan was most likely to sexually assault the victims somewhere private and quiet (if such a place could be found) once he had got them off the train and then flee afterwards. While this plan was slightly more plausible than attempting to abduct the women Frederick Clegg style and take them home, it was still unrealistic and betrayed the fact that, even at this early point in his life, Plumb was rapidly losing his grasp on reality and allowing fantasy to cloud his thoughts.

Gavin Plumb's later plan to abduct Holly Willoughby, whether he intended to really do it or not, had something in common with the criminal train incidents in that it was never very realistic. He was an overweight man with no car and little money. The alleged accomplices he was in contact with to abduct Holly Willoughby were just people online that he'd never met. He didn't even know most of their real names and none of them were stupid enough to actually go and meet Plumb in real life.

The question of whether Gavin Plumb thought the Holly Willoughby plan was stupid and just a fantasy was more complex. It would need a trial to put that to the test. But the prosecution in 2024 were given valuable ammunition by these frightening air-stewardess train incidents from 2007. Plumb's train abduction plan, like his Holly Willoughby plan, was stupid and unrealistic but he'd still gone ahead with it hadn't he? This was exactly what the prosecution would say in 2024. Thankfully (and perhaps predictably) neither of the train abduction attempts by Gavin Plumb were successful. The first woman (who spoke to the media years later when Gavin Plumb became infamous) had started crying when Plumb threatened her and other passengers eventually noticed this and came over to help.

The first woman Plumb tried to abduct was a French stewardess who worked for Ryanair and was on her way to work. This woman's real name was never revealed, She had her identity protected in the much later press interview - in which she said that Gavin Plumb could have been stopped much sooner if he'd been given a harsher sentence for his initial crimes. The air-stewardess was on her way to work but hadn't done her make-up yet so she was attending to that on the train. She said she could sense straight away that Plumb was bad news the moment he shuffled into view on the carriage. As soon as she saw him she was creeped out.

When he sat down next to the stewardess, Plumb put his hand on her leg. The stewardess was absolutely terrified and almost frozen in fear. "There was this moment when I was frozen and scared. But it was also disbelief, I thought maybe he is joking, it is absurd, but he started approaching me with his hands, he held his hand on my knee and he was indicating that 'we are going to go'. After the initial freeze and disbelief I realised what's going on and I was frightened, that feeling was growing because I started realising that this massive man wants to get me off the train and I knew the next station is in a small village."

The train carriage was empty at the time - which had obviously emboldened Plumb - but thankfully another passenger came into view and the stewardess was able to attract help. The stewardess described herself as very petite and said the sheer size of Plumb was terrifying because she knew he could easily overpower her if he chose to do that. Gavin Plumb had a replica gun and a piece of rope and had handed the woman a note telling her to get off at the next station - which was a fairly quiet station often bereft of people or staff. She had though thankfully managed in the end to attract the attention of another female passenger who came into view and this passenger then went to ask a male passenger for help. Plumb noticed this was happening and fled.

The note Plumb had given the victim read - 'I have got a gun. All you have to do is keep quiet. Do what I say. So just stand up and get off at the next stop with me. Don't cry or make a sound. Don't stop me from touching you, because I won't hurt you. If you do all of this, no one will get hurt. But if you don't, I'm going to shoot you and myself and everyone else.' Both of the abduction attempts were broadly similar. Plumb even pretended to be a police officer for the second of these incidents - not that this fooled the potential victim. He had shown his patently fake ID very quickly and then hidden it. He told the air-stewardess that other police officers were waiting at the next station to talk to her. Plumb was a shabby overweight young man. He looked nothing like a police officer and so the victim didn't believe him for a second.

You'd like to think that it would be impossible to threaten women on a train and get away with it and happily, in this case at least, that's what happened. Plumb was picked up by Transport Police after being reported by the second air-stewardess and taken into custody. The fact that he wasn't picked up after the first incident was somewhat perplexing. Though he obviously had to get off the train at the station, he was able to leave the scene and go home without being arrested. Once he was in custody, Gavin Plumb told the police that the replica gun in his pocket was from his little brother. He said his little brother often pretended to be a police officer with a fake gun and borrowed his coat whenever he did this. Plumb suggested his brother must have unwittingly left the fake gun in the coat. Suffice to say, this preposterous and desperate lie didn't convince anyone.

Gavin Plumb, like most fantasists, was a very unconvincing liar. He was capable of the most childlike ridiculous lies. We would see more evidence of this later on in 2024 - culminating in his brazenly preposterous and laughable claim to the court that he had purchased two bottles of chloroform to clean a stain on his carpet. Gavin Plumb would later claim he knew he would be arrested for these train abduction incidents and that's why he did them. He said they were a cry for help because he was in a toxic relationship (this was obviously Laura Roberts) and wanted to get himself arrested as a way out. That explanation was weak and bizarre to say the least. Many people experience relationship trouble but they don't go around with plastic guns trying to abduct people on trains as a consequence!

We can see then already that Gavin Plumb was a strange and dangerous character and a terrible liar to boot. We can see that he was capable of awful things. The French air-stewardess who Plumb tried to abduct said she chose not to reveal her identity because she didn't want her name to be connected to him. "You do not want your name to be attached to a person like Gavin Plumb and this is one reason I want to remain anonymous. I do not want to be associated with him in any way. He has in my eyes, he has nothing in life. It makes him in a way more dangerous, you know a person who has nothing to lose. No ability to control himself. I almost feel pity for him."

For these train crimes, Plumb pleaded guilty to two counts of attempted kidnap and was later sentenced to a prison term of twelve months - suspended for two years, with supervision and activity requirements. All in all, he got off lightly given the gravity of his offences and how much he had terrified the victims. The French air-stewardess said she had a lot of trouble trusting men again after the incident. If she encountered a man she didn't know she automatically feared the worst thanks to her harrowing experience with Gavin Plumb. There is certainly an argument that the modest sentence for the train incidents actually encouraged rather than discouraged Plumb when it came to his attempted sex offending and criminal activities. He had tried to abduct two women and yet hardly seemed to be punished for that at all.

There is a very obvious theory that the light sentence made Gavin Plumb feel invincible and as if he could get away with anything. A twelve month suspended sentence for trying to abduct two women on a train doesn't sound like too much of a deterrent to the committed sex offender. In his later online communications in the Holly Willoughby/celebrity abduction themed groups, Plumb actually mocked the justice system at one point and seemed to make light of the fact he was not given much of a sentence for his past crimes.

Gavin Plumb's claim that he had threatened these women on the train and tried to abduct them because he wanted to get arrested and escape from a toxic relationship obviously made no sense whatsoever. If you really wanted to get yourself arrested there are a great many more harmless things you could do to arrange that. The most obvious would be to steal something from a shop. Plumb though chose to try and abduct two women on a train.

Plainly, his claim that he had done this purely to get arrested was a lie. If he had done this on purpose why he didn't he hand himself in at the police station or choose a much busier train (where he would have been apprehended much more swiftly)? He had done this because it was his biggest sexual fantasy at the time. Plumb had no desire to get arrested. All he desired was to abduct or molest an airline stewardess. Anything else beyond that did not concern him. He gave no thought to that at all. Many abductors seek power over their victims. This desire for control can stem from feelings of inadequacy or powerlessness in their own lives. For some, the act of abduction provides a sense of thrill or excitement. This can be associated with certain personality disorders, such as Antisocial Personality Disorder. A sense of superiority or entitlement might drive some abductors like Plumb, making them view others as mere objects or obstacles.

It was also absurd for Plumb to try and portray himself as some sort of victim in his relationship with Laura Roberts when the opposite was true. His attempt to portray himself as the victim in this relationship was right up there with his most shameless lies. Gavin Plumb initially told the police that these train incidents were merely 'pranks' because he was bored - which was yet another obvious untruth. Going up to a terrified woman on a train, handing her a threatening note, pretending to have a gun, and fondling her knee is not what you would describe as a prank. Amazingly though, as we have seen, Plumb was barely punished for these incidents at all. A judge ruled that his offences were at the 'lower end' of the scale - which was a rather strange way to describe sexual harassment and attempted abduction.

Rather than a serious prison sentence, Plumb's time on remand was taken into account and he was also ordered to go on a course aimed at stopping people from offending again. This was the Think First programme (TFP). Think First was designed to treat impulsivity and criminal thinking. Whatever the success rate of this programme it is safe to say it didn't do much good for Gavin Plumb. That was basically then the extent of Gavin Plumb's punishment for terrifying two women on a train. A brief spell in prison and being put on a course. Laura Roberts said she spoke to Gavin Plumb while he was (briefly) in prison and initially stood by him. Plumb somehow convinced her that he'd been falsely convicted of these crimes and was innocent - which obviously wasn't true at all.

At this young point in his life Gavin Plumb had already told more lies than Aldridge Prior. This was the last time though that Laura Roberts would refuse to believe the worst about Gavin Plumb. The next time he got into trouble she wasn't surprised at all. Laura also soon realised that the train convictions were assuredly not false. Laura Roberts finally left Gavin Plumb for good in 2008 after contacting the police. She accused Plumb of rape. Laura said the police did not pursue her rape allegation because they said they didn't have enough evidence. That turned out to be a big mistake by the police because it left Gavin Plumb free to commit further crimes against women. Laura Roberts only had one aim now. To take her children and get as far away from Gavin Plumb as possible. She didn't want Plumb to have any influence at all over her kids and she wanted out of this controlling, abusive, and horrible relationship.

The loss of Laura Roberts and his children, though it was allegedly what he had wanted (well, the loss of Laura at least) according to Gavin Plumb, left Plumb adrift in the world. Plumb had his supportive parents and siblings but it obviously wasn't the same as having a partner and children. To fill this void in his life, Gavin Plumb began to descend once again into dangerous fantasy. His darkest sexual desires began to dominate his thoughts. Plumb's desire to abduct someone as his own plaything hadn't gone away. In fact, these desires were stronger than other. The Think First programme (TFP) that Plumb had completed after his train convictions proved to be a spectacular failure in this specific case. Gavin Plumb hadn't changed at all. He emerged from prison more dangerous than when he went in. In a matter of months he resumed his fledgling career as an incompetent but frightening and unhinged abductor of women and the place he chose to do this next time was truly bizarre.

In 2008, the 21 year-old Gavin Plumb, despite his criminal convictions for terrifying two women on a train, somehow managed to get a job at his local Woolworths store in Harlow as a shop assistant. Staff who worked with him at Woolworths later said he would sweat a lot and his body odour was so bad that the store manager would secretly and strategically deploy air fresheners around the areas where Plumb worked so that the unwitting customers didn't have to endure the undiluted horror of Plumb's overpowering smell. Plumb's duties included restocking the shelves and also working on the till. Some of the other staff who worked with Plumb at Woolworths were teenage girls. It was, in hindsight, an obvious recipe for disaster and - sure enough - Gavin Plumb was soon back to his old (or not so old in this case) ways.

Whoever decided to place Gavin Plumb in an environment where he shared work shifts with young women had either not looked at his criminal convictions or simply chose to ignore them. It could be the case that someone decided Plumb would not be a danger at Woolworths because it was a store full of staff and cameras and no one would be stupid enough to try and harass or molest a woman in a store full of staff and cameras would they? Maybe they just presumed Gavin Plumb had been rehabilitated and thought that a job would be good for him and keep him on the straight and narrow. Whatever the reasoning or logic for handing Plumb this unexpected employment opportunity, it all turned out to be a very big mistake.

Sixteen year-old Emma Ashby worked some of the same shifts as Gavin Plumb. Emma was working at Woolworths part-time and had just started further education college to study childcare. Emma later said she had done some of her staff training course with Plumb and he'd seemed harmless and normal enough. That neutral opinion was soon to change though drastically thanks to a terrifying encounter with Gavin Plumb in an empty warehouse stockroom. One night, had Emma arranged for her friend Louise (who was also sixteen) to work a trial shift with her as Louise also wanted some part-time work. The two girls were excited to have a part-time job because it would give them a little bit of financial independence and spending money for the first time in their lives.

Emma occasionally worked the till next to Plumb on her shifts and described him as coming across as quite friendly. She said they'd engaged in some small talk before on the tills but he wasn't a big talker or very outgoing. Although he was only 21, Plumb could have passed for a man in his thirties and so he seemed ancient to the sixteen year-old Emma Ashby. Plumb and Emma were not what you would describe as work friends. Emma said she knew nothing about Gavin Plumb. She had no idea where he lived, if he had a wife or girlfriend, or what he did outside of work. She also had no idea about his criminal convictions and was completely unaware that Plumb had once tried to abduct two women. He was just some bloke who worked in the same store that she would occasionally say hello to.

Emma said that Gavin Plumb was a big man who was clearly carrying a few too many extra pounds but he wasn't outrageously overweight at the time. In the press photographs she later saw of him (thanks to the Holly Willoughby case) Plumb seemed huge and obese compared to the 21 year-old Plumb she remembered briefly knowing years ago. Emma said that Plumb wasn't especially tall but he still seemed quite imposing to her as far as height goes because she was only 5'1. The fateful shift that Emma and Louise were working was five to nine in the evening so the store was closed. Their basic duties were to replenish the shelves of the shop floor department they had been assigned to. This meant frequent trips to the stockroom. It was nearing Christmas and there were Christmas songs playing in the store. The two girls were wearing Santa hats and getting into the festive spirit. They were joking around and having a nice time. The happy Christmas atmosphere was about to be shattered though in a most unexpected and frightening fashion.

Emma and her friend Louise went to the warehouse stockroom to replenish the shelves on the shop floor. The two girls had to take stuff from the stockroom and put it on a trolley to take to the shop floor and then keep repeating the process. This was after hours. Gavin Plumb, who was obviously one of the other staff working this shift, offered to help Emma and Louise lift down some heavy boxes containing cans of soft fizzy drinks. The boxes were a bit too heavy and high up for the girls to safely lift down themselves so they needed some assistance. Gavin Plumb did not help them lift the boxes down from the shelf though. What he did instead was completely unexpected and shocking.

The girls were surprised (to say the least) when Plumb

suddenly brandished a six-inch knife (which he'd taken from a box on the shop floor - it was a kitchen knife according to Emma and not a Stanley knife as is sometimes reported) and waved it at them in a threatening manner akin to a mugger about to rob someone. There was a strange look on Plumb's face. It was as if his entire personality had changed. He was suddenly blank and unemotional. Plumb then barked at the two girls to go to the back of the stockroom and face the wall. The two girls thought this was all a prank at first and had even laughed initially. It was a very surreal moment.

Plumb responded by once again barking at the girls to go to the back of the stockroom and face the wall. There was more force in his voice this time. He wasn't joking at all. Emma and Louise looked at one another and in that horrible and terrifying moment realised this was actually real. It was a chilling moment for the two teenagers because it now dawned on them that the previously quiet, unassuming and incredibly large man working the same shift as them was in fact a dangerous lunatic and sexual predator. The two girls ran to the back of the wall away from Plumb and he walked over to them. Emma was shaking in fear. Plumb had some tape and rope on him. Suffice to say, hiring a man with criminal convictions for attempting to abduct women on a train and then putting him on a shift with teenage girls wasn't the smartest move in the world. Who was to blame for this? The parole officers? The court? Woolworths?

Emma said she recalled Plumb pulling the rope from his pocket but becoming frustrated because it was all tangled. So he had thrown the rope on the floor and switched to the roll of tape he had. The tape was in the same pocket as the rope. Plumb told the two girls to face the wall so he could tie their hands up behind them with tape. Emma said that Plumb issued his instructions in a very aggressive and frightening way. Just as Plumb was attempting to put tape around Emma's mouth, Louise managed to make a run for it. Gavin Plumb, purely on instinct, then broke away to go after Louise and this in turn gave Emma a chance to run away too. Once the two fleet-footed girls were free and had space to run into it was almost impossible for the lumbering clumsy giant who had tried to restrain them to catch up.

Emma was able to activate the stockroom door key code and then make it to the shop floor to alert other staff. Emma later said that Plumb had actually changed his usual shifts so he would be working with her that evening. This indicated that he had planned this attack all in advance and it was something he had been contemplating and thinking about for quite a while. Emma ran through the middle of the shop floor shouting. Other staff were then alerted by Emma - who was understandably distressed and tearful by this stage - once she escaped from the clutches of Gavin Plumb and made it to the shop floor. Emma told them that her friend Louise was still trapped with Plumb so two male members of staff went to investigate. Thankfully, Louise appeared a few moments later and although greatly shaken by her experience had not been harmed.

The staff made sure the two girls were safe and then called the police and also the parents of Emma and Louise. Gavin Plumb meanwhile had put the knife back in the box in the kitchen department from where he took it and gone back to the area he was previously working before he tried to assault the girls. He was basically, in a very childlike sort of way, trying to pretend nothing had happened. Other staff watched over Plumb while they waited for the police to arrive. Emma later said that she can't remember seeing Plumb be taken away by the police. She may have left by that point. That terrifying encounter in the stockroom was the last time she ever spoke to Gavin Plumb.

Emma recalled spending many hours in the police station afterwards giving statements. She said in the media years later that when she read that Plumb had said during his 2024 trial that he had felt 'scared' when he tried to restrain the two girls at Woolworths she was outraged because she knew it was a blatant lie. Emma said that Plumb wasn't scared in the least when he attacked her and Louise. He hadn't shown the slightest inkling of fear or nerves. Gavin Plumb pled guilty to two counts of false imprisonment for the attack on Emma and Louise and was jailed for 32 months. He served 16 months of the sentence in prison. There was also a restraining order preventing Plumb from going anywhere near Emma Ashby and Louise when he got out of prison. He was the last person they ever wanted to clap eyes on again. Plumb was also banned from working with anyone under the age of eighteen.

Emma Ashby did not give evidence in court for the Woolworths incident but she turn up to watch Gavin Plumb being sentenced. She saw that Plumb's entire family were there to support him as if he'd done nothing wrong. Emma said she heard that Plumb told a pack of lies in court - the most ludicrous of which was Plumb claiming that Emma Ashby 'fancied' him. Emma barely knew Plumb and found him fairly repulsive so this was plainly a preposterous fiction invented by Plumb. Emma said she was very shocked when she found out that Plumb had previously tried to abduct two airline-stewardesses because it seemed insane to her that a man could be convicted of crimes like this and then get a job at Woolworths working with teenage girls. Did no one do any background checks on who they were hiring?

Emma Ashby said she wasn't surprised at all when Gavin Plumb's name became public in relation to the Holly Willoughby kidnap case - though Plumb was someone she hadn't thought about for a good few years. Emma had first hand experience of what an unhinged and dangerous man Plumb truly was. It was no surprise to Emma that Gavin Plumb seemed to remain a dangerous and disturbed person. Emma Ashby was asked to give a statement for Plumb's trial in 2024 but in the end it wasn't used in court. Emma Ashby later suggested that the months of planning Plumb seemed to put into his Holly Willoughby abduction obsession was a consequence of the fact that his previous abduction attempts hadn't gone very well and showed little sign of any advance planning. Emma believed that Plumb wanted to rectify his past mistakes and research the abduction more thoroughly this time. This was also a theme that the prosecution in 2024 would mine in court with a fair degree of success.

You'd think Plumb would have learned his lesson after the train convictions but Woolworths proved he evidently hadn't. There are of course theories that his light sentence for the train incidents and being spoilt by his mother as a child made him think he could get away with anything. The reality is probably less complicated. It seems that Plumb's sexual desires and abduction fantasies were things he couldn't suppress or control at this time. They short-circuited his brain and made him do crazy and horrible things.

Gavin Plumb no longer had the ability to stop and think about the consequences of his actions. All he cared about where the actions themselves. He simply didn't think beyond that. When he got the job at Woolworths, Plumb didn't count himself lucky and decide to get his head down and make the best of this opportunity. What he did instead was notice that he shared shifts with teenage girls - girls who could be easily isolated in stock warehouses.

Gavin Plumb's latest and craziest (did he really think he was going to get away with assaulting two co-workers in a Woolworths stockroom?) abduction attempt was thankfully over not long after it began. Despite his previous convictions he hadn't changed at all. Plumb didn't even have the ridiculous excuse this time of pretending that he had done this to get arrested so he could escape from his 'toxic' relationship because there was no tangible relationship to escape from anymore. Emma and Louise were greatly affected by their harrowing ordeal and found it difficult to trust people again for a while. When you are at work you assume you are in a safe environment. The last thing you expect is to be attacked by a co-worker. Emma Ashby said that in the end she refused to let Gavin Plumb affect her life so she simply chose to forget about him. She is now a mother and lives a happy life.

When he got out of prison, Gavin Plumb spent some time sleeping on sofas living with his brother and also his parents because he didn't have a place of his own and he didn't have any money. It took him a while to get fixed up with a council flat. It was amazing really that such a young man already had two convictions for similar crimes and equally amazing that his punishments for these crimes had amounted to so little. By now, Laura Roberts, the mother of Plumb's children was long gone. She moved to Great Yarmouth with her kids and had a restraining order against Gavin Plumb. Laura Roberts later told the media that in 2010 Plumb once tracked her down in Great Yarmouth and threatened her, telling his ex-partner to 'watch her back'. Laura Roberts said that Plumb was angered by not having contact with his children. Laura Roberts was one person who never had any doubt that Gavin Plumb's celebrity abduction plan was something he would have carried out. Laura said that if Gavin Plumb could track her down a 100 miles away in Great Yarmouth then he could certainly track down Holly Willoughby.

It was around this time that, lonely and as usual at a loose end, Gavin Plumb began using the internet much more to talk to people. Plumb worked as a kitchen assistant at Pizza Hut between 2011 and 2012 - where it is said that he piled on more weight thanks to the free food on offer. As ever, his employment was not destined to last very long.

On his LinkedIn profile, Plumb listed himself as a 'Restaurants Professional' - which was a bit of an exaggeration. Plumb moved to Waltham Abbey in 2013 though as usual he was something of an enigma to his neighbours. Most of them said they rarely saw him and he sat indoors with the curtains shut all day. Plumb had been mobile enough up to this point of his life to get employment and threaten women. This would soon no longer be possible in the end - at least for a time. His weight was gradually starting to get out of control and his criminal convictions were not exactly a great help when it came to finding work.

Plumb's isolation and lack of employment drew him ever closer to the dark corners of the internet. Frustrated by lack of success with women and the failure of his abduction and sexual assault activities, Plumb fantasies and energies found a natural home in the grungy and cruddy world of private internet chat groups where you could say anything you wanted - no matter how dark. This was where Gavin Plumb now increasingly spent most of his time. Plumb's internet history displayed a disturbing obsession with reading about real life rape cases. What it also showed was an obsessive interest in famous female celebrities and violent fantasies about them. Plumb was fascinated by deep fake pictures of celebrities - especially ones which showed them tied up. He had tried and failed to abduct women in the real world but his ultimate fantasy was to abduct a female celebrity. But was this merely a fantasy or something he actually intended to do one day?

CHAPTER THREE

A young woman who lived in the flat next to Gavin Plumb when he was in Harlow later said the only time she ever heard any noise was when he was watching football. Apart from that you could hear a pin drop on the other side of the wall. The woman said that Plumb rarely had any guests at his flat and so spent a lot of time alone. These guests were most likely his mother and stepfather and some of his siblings. Wherever he lived, Plumb tended to keep himself to himself and spend most of his time engrossed in his internet surfing and online chatting. Some of Plumb's reclusive nature was involuntary in that he was for long periods too heavy and unfit to go anywhere but even when he was more mobile he didn't get out much. The only time he went out out on a regular basis was when he had employment and so had no choice but to leave the house each day.

Plumb was not workshy and his long periods of unemployment were not through choice. If there was a job available to him and he was fit enough to work he would take the job. Employment was obviously difficult to attain for Plumb though because of his lack of qualifications, limited work experience, poor health, and (last but by no means least) criminal record. Plumb lived on the ground floor in Harlow but in Waltham Abbey he had a second floor flat. One of his neighbours said the only time he ever saw Gavin Plumb was when Plumb briefly had a job and used to wait outside the building for a taxi to take him to work in the morning. The neighbour said the last time he saw Gavin Plumb was when Plumb was being led away in handcuffs by the police in 2023.

Gavin Plumb rarely spoke to his neighbours. He was not a very social person and not the type to befriend those who lived around him. Plumb usually joined online residents associations (and then never contributed to discussions) but that was about the extent of his community spirit. Plumb could occasionally be seen by neighbours having a smoke by his bin when he put the rubbish bag out or having phone conversations just outside of his flat but sightings of him were few. In the end a sighting of Gavin Plumb by neighbours became as rare as Bigfoot or the Loch Ness Monster. Gavin Plumb had lost interest in reality and retreated into the synthetic world of online friends.

A number of his former neighbours spoke to the media in the wake of Plumb's 2024 conviction - a conviction which briefly made Gavin Plumb headline news. None of them had anything nice to say about him. One of his neighbours, who was a young mother at the time she lived near him, said she was very annoyed when Gavin Plumb put CCTV cameras on his window and door. She found this creepy because Plumb would be collecting footage of her and her children as they went about their daily business. When she complained to Plumb about the cameras he said he had put them there because he had a 'crazy' ex-partner he was worried about. This was clearly a lie. The only real ex-partner he had was Laura Roberts and she wasn't crazy. Laura was also happily getting on with her life a hundred miles away so she was hardly a nuisance to Plumb.

During the 2024 trial, the prosecution argued that Plumb had set up these CCTV cameras in preparation for keeping Holly Willoughby captive in his flat. Plumb's abduction plan, at some point at least (it tended to change from time to time), involved 'stashing' Holly Willoughby in his flat as a temporary measure before she could be moved to somewhere more remote. Gavin Plumb denied that the CCTV cameras were in preparation for an abduction but it did seem strange that someone living in a small council flat should require such extensive security. The fact that Gavin Plumb actually purchased items (like CCTV cameras, metal cable ties, restraints, chloroform etc) which would plainly have been helpful in an abduction was something the prosecution also zeroed in on during the 2024 trial. If his abduction plan was just an online fantasy why was he spending money on these things?

Aside from the internet and watching football, Gavin Plumb's main hobby was food. Plumb loved junk food and he was also addicted to full sugar cocoa-cola - which he guzzled in enormous quantities. Plumb was using food to plug the emptiness of his life and his weight grew to dangerous proportions. Plumb later said that, when he was at his heaviest, a doctor told him if he didn't lose weight he'd be dead within four years. Plumb was 35 stone at one point. To put that in perspective, this made him well over fifteen stones heavier than the 6'9 heavyweight boxer Tyson Fury. Plumb's ballooning weight made his reclusive nature not a lifestyle choice but a forced one. He could barely stand up let alone leave the flat and go outside and it was impossible for him to work. Plumb was huge. He desperately needed to do something before it was too late.

His weight problems did though lead to a very minor and unexpected brush with fame. Plumb appeared on the BBC news website in 2018 in relation to a piece about obesity. He had texted BBC Radio 5 Live's Afternoon Edition programme in 2016 talking about his weight problem and so the BBC kept in touch and used him for the health item about obesity. The BBC evidently (one would presume) did not know that they were talking to a convicted two-time sex offender who had once threatened two teenagers with a knife and then tried to restrain them with tape. Plumb clearly enjoyed getting this attention from the BBC. It must have felt like the closest he would ever get to being a celebrity.

Of course, in the end Gavin Plumb's appearance on the BBC website was quickly forgotten and he then made headlines around the world for being the lunatic who apparently wanted to abduct Holly Willoughby. Plumb became a celebrity in the end - but only a weird minor true crime celebrity who became a footnote in the life of a famous television presenter.

Gavin Plumb told the BBC he had been waiting four years to have gastric band surgery and was desperate to lose some weight. He just wanted to go outside and play football again. Plumb said he was in constant pain because of his weight and it was a struggle to even reach his front door let alone go outside. The only exercise he got was when he put his rubbish out on the balcony to be collected and even this was a struggle. He was determined to change his life and that meant losing some of the weight.

"My weight has always fluctuated," Plumb told the BBC. "At my heaviest, I was 35-and-a-half stone. When the weight started to pile on, that was when my mental health really went down. I'm pretty much in pain everywhere. I get chest pains and I've just been told it's because of my weight. The last time I went out unaided was 2014 — it was my parents' wedding vow renewal. I hate sitting indoors. I hate looking at the same four walls 24/7. I hate being the size I am. My parents are absolutely fantastic. They come over and help tidy up - but I know they worry. My mum worries that they're going to come over and she's going to find me on the floor, dead from a heart attack. I've given both my parents keys, not only for the security door downstairs but for my front door as well, just in case."

Gavin Plumb came across as very sympathetic and likeable in the BBC article and short interview clips. A plucky chap going through a lot to try to get his weight under control. There were half a dozen women out there though who would have been less than sympathetic had they chanced upon Gavin Plumb's BBC interview. "I used to drink 18 litres of cola (36 pints) over a week and a half," Plumb told the BBC. "But I stopped drinking it completely. And I cut out sugar and put sweeteners in my tea. I've gone on diets before but I've always put the weight back on. This time, I had support." Plumb had gastric band surgery in 2018. While he was not exactly svelte afterwards and wouldn't be running any marathons anytime soon, he did manage to shed some of the pounds through a liquid diet and avoiding sugar and junk food.

Gastric band surgery basically restricts how much food you can eat and makes you feel full up much sooner. Plumb was in hospital for four days after the surgery. It was supposed to be two days but Plumb had some problems with his breathing and was kept in for a couple of extra days so he could remain under observation. The liquid diet was compulsory after this surgery and then he was permitted to eat 'soft food' for a time. This meant that Plumb had to eat things like scrambled egg and mashed potato (which wasn't much fun) until he was finally allowed to go back to a full normal diet. Plumb said he had learned his lesson and would eat healthy food from now on. He never wanted to be 35 stone again because that had been agony. The surgery was a success in that some of the weight finally started to come off.

Ordinary simple things that we all take for granted, like putting on some shoes, having a shower or bath, and even using the toilet, had once been a struggle for Plumb but now he felt like he was starting to get some control of his life back. He was more mobile and no longer in constant pain. The weight loss meant he was able to look for work again. From his high of 35 stones, Plumb managed to lose eleven stones by the time of his trial in 2024. While he was still a huge man in comparison to most people even after the gastric band surgery, Gavin Plumb must have felt as skinny as a rake compared to how he used to be. He was walking around again without pain and his breathing and sleep was much better. The prosecution at the 2024 trial would claim that there was an ulterior motive for Gavin Plumb's determination to lose weight. They argued that he didn't just want to lose weight for health reasons. They believed that a big part of his motivation was that he wanted to be fit and mobile enough to start trying to abduct women again.

Gavin Plumb's flat was small and slightly messy but it wasn't a Dennis Nilsen style hovel. It wasn't absurdly cluttered and he wasn't a hoarder. He had some DVDs and games on a shelf and a Ghostbusters symbol was evident in photographs. Plumb had a Liverpool football club mat in his hall and was a big Liverpool fan. He once posted an online video of himself (tunelessly and dreadfully) singing You'll Never Walk Alone. This was basically where Gavin Plumb's life was at this point. With absolutely nothing to do all day he was reduced to trying to carve out some sort of substitute life online rather than the real world. That would have been perfectly fine if he'd stuck to making terrible singing videos and playing Call of Duty video games. Sadly he didn't though. He would eventually plunge deeper and deeper in the worst aspects of the internet and for this he would pay a very heavy price. With nothing to do, Plumb had increasingly fallen down down the rabbit hole of fantasy.

Gavin Plumb, thanks to being housebound due to his weight and then unemployed for a period, watched a lot of daytime television to pass the time. One show he never missed was the daily ITV magazine show This Morning. Though he could never have guessed it at the time, This Morning would prove to be his ultimate downfall. This Morning was what you might describe as undemanding background wallpaper television. It was there on ITV each morning and viewers dipped in and out as the show juggled showbiz fluff and celebrity gossip, medical matters, cooking segments, an Agony Aunt, topical issues, competitions, and interviewed celebrities with a new show or book they were contractually obliged to go out and plug. This Morning first began decades ago in 1988 and was originally based at Liverpool Docks and hosted by the husband and wife presenting team of Richard Madeley and Judy Finnegan. Having a live show of this type on in the morning was fairly new in 1988.

This Morning with Richard & Judy quickly became cultish with a sizeable audience of students, unemployed people, and housewives - plus a few house husbands too no doubt. Because there were only four channels and the internet wasn't a thing yet, television shows in the late 1980s and early 1990s had big viewing figures in comparison to today. One of the most famous parts of the show came when This Morning's enthusiastic weatherman Fred Talbot would do the weather forecast standing on a giant map of the British Isles which was perched in the water outside the studio. Everyone always waited excitedly for the moment when he would have to carefully jump over to Ireland without falling in. He always managed to do this but everyone still watched in the hope that Talbot might one day come a cropper and get soaked. The format of This Morning proved to be durable and successful. The presenters would change but the actual show stayed more or less the same as it had always been.

As ever with a long running show, things changed on This Morning. It moved from Liverpool Docks to a London studio by the Thames in 1996. ITV made the change because they said it was very difficult to find celebrity guests willing to trek up to Liverpool for a ten minute interview. Richard Madeley and Judy Finnegan moved on and there was a revolving door of new presenters - some more successful than others. As for Fred Talbot with his madcap weather map antics, well, he ended up in prison when it came to light that he'd sexually abused boys in his former occupation of teacher. Despite all the changes, This Morning remained a seemingly indestructible pillar of ITV's weekly morning schedules. There are now entire generations of viewers today who can't remember a time when This Morning wasn't on the telly.

The main reason why Gavin Plumb watched This Morning was assuredly not because he enjoyed the soap gossip, reality television updates, and 'issue of the day' phone ins. Plumb was addicted to This Morning for one reason and one reason only. He was completely besotted with the current regular co-host of the show - the blonde haired Holly Willoughby. Holly Willoughby first joined This Morning in 2009 and the presenting duo of Willoughby and Phillip Schofield eventually became as famous as Richard & Judy had been in the show's early days. Holly Willoughby seemed like someone who had been bio engineered in a top secret ITV science lab purely for task of hosting a daytime magazine show like This Morning. She was the perfect host for this sort of show. Shows of this type live or die (where the ratings are concerned) on the popularity and chemistry of the presenters. This Morning, as far as daytime morning fluff goes, seemed to strike gold in Holly Willoughby and Schofield. They had the believable chemistry of genuine friends and seemed to be having a good time. These qualities translated to the audience watching at home.

Holly Willoughby was born on February 10, 1981, in Brighton. Willoughby went to Burgess Hill Girls school - a private independent school. Her dad was a double glazing businessman and her mum was (in what can perhaps be seen as darkly ironic in hindsight) an airline stewardess. Holly Willoughby was first spotted by a model scout at The Clothes Show Live in 1995. She was only about fourteen at the time. She was signed by Storm Model management and appeared as a model in teen magazines for girls like More!, Mizz and Just Seventeen. Her first television appearance came playing a young woman in an advert for bra brand Pretty Polly. Willoughby 'graduated' to these types of underwear ads when she hit seventeen/eighteen. You can be pretty certain that Gavin Plumb must have done a fair few web searches in relation to Willoughby's underwear model days.

Holly Willoughby cashed in on her wholesome good looks and sex appeal when she was younger and had a long association with FHM magazine - becoming a permanent fixture in the magazine's annual 100 Sexiest Women poll. Holly Willoughby was shrewd enough though to realise that she couldn't do underwear adverts and racy magazine photoshoots for the rest of her life. There was only a short window for the type of model work that Willoughby did. There was a constant supply of younger women coming up behind her to be models for magazines and underwear adverts so Holly Willoughby began to carve out a presenting career on television. She proved to be highly successful in this new goal - so successful in fact that it would be hard to think of a female presenter today who is as famous as Holly Willoughby in Britain. In 2004, Willoughby landed her first major role as a presenter on the children's show Ministry of Mayhem. Among the other shows she has presented are Xtra Factor and Dancing On Ice.

In no time at all, Willoughby was one of the most familiar faces on British television. It wasn't just This Morning where Gavin Plumb got his Holly Willoughby 'fix' because she was also on shows like I'm a Celebrity...Get Me Out of Here! and Celebrity Juice. Holly Willoughby began on This Morning as a replacement for Fern Britton but quickly made the job on the show her own and so most of the viewers soon (with respect) forgot all about Fern Britton. Viewing figures for This Morning increased by 20% when Holly Willoughby became a regular presenter. ITV had hit the jackpot by recruiting Willoughby. Away from the camera, Willoughby married the television producer Dan Baldwin and they had three children together - Harry, Belle, and Chester. Outside of her television career, Willoughby is also a successful author, having written books about parenting and fashion.

Aside from the lad's mag photoshoots when she was younger, Holly Willoughby avoided the slightly trashier aspects of celebrity culture. She was more of the stylish and slightly out of reach girl next door than someone who wobbled out of nightclubs at 4 in the morning or got embroiled in tabloid scandals. Though sometimes portrayed as bland or a bimbo by armchair internet television critics, there is no question that Holly Willoughby's career was a masterful operation. She has over eight million Instagram followers and a reported net worth of £12 million. Not bad for someone who started their career as a model in teen magazines. Holly Willoughby's main focus was on family life and she was said to be very down to earth and normal away from the cameras. Willoughby was often seen taking a weekend stroll with her kids in South West London and it was said that she even drove herself to work (a fact which was apparently not lost on Gavin Plumb).

Holly Willoughby posted a lot of photographs on social media of happy family scenes in her home and garden and you can be certain that Gavin Plumb would have avidly trawled through these updates from afar. A little glimpse, however mundane, into the private life of Holly Willoughby would have been very exciting to Plumb you'd imagine. Holly Willoughby continued hosting This Morning for many years. There she was each morning, now in her forties, ever smiling, seemingly ageless. She even outlasted Phillip Schofield - who eventually left the show for well publicised reasons that have nothing to do with the subject matter of this book. Holly Willoughby steadied the This Morning ship after Schofield's unexpected departure though and looked set to carry on hosting the show forever until the end of time. Little did she know that her days on This Morning were now numbered and coming to an end. All thanks to a certain man in Essex by the name of Gavin Plumb.

Meanwhile, Gavin Plumb, now that he'd lost some weight and was more mobile than he had been for a good few years, was starting to have those old familiar urges about abducting or molesting someone. His targets in the past had been air stewardesses on trains and two co-workers at Woolworths. Now though the seed of a crazy new idea was beginning to form in his troubled head. Plumb began to have dark fantasies about abducting a famous female celebrity and keeping her captive as his own personal property. The person that he fantasised most of all about abducting and 'owning' was Holly Willoughby. Plumb had long since moved past the relatively harmless 'celebrity crush' phase of this interest in Willoughby and allowed it to morph into a very unhealthy obsession.

Because he was often unemployed and rarely went outside, Plumb spent most of his time either on his games console, phone, the internet, or watching television. Fantasy offers an escape from the sometimes harsh realities of everyday life, allowing us to imagine a world where anything is possible. However, when fantasy begins to overshadow reality it can lead to trouble. Gavin Plumb seemed to get fantasy and reality confused in the end. He didn't seem to realise they do not exist in the same universe. There is sometimes a theory that stalkers or nutty fans become obsessed with celebrities because they see them in their homes on television and this makes them (mistakenly) think they have some sort of special personal connection to that celebrity that no one else shares.

While this may have applied to some stalking cases it didn't seem applicable to Gavin Plumb (who wasn't really a stalker anyway). Plumb was clearly a horrible and troubled person but he wasn't disturbed enough to believe that Holly Willoughby was sending him coded messages through his television screen as she hosted This Morning. Plumb's interest in Holly Willoughby did though become all consuming - to the point where his fantasy about abducting her had more or less taken over his whole life. In the end it was all he would think about and dominated his online activities. Though he did not know it at the time, this obsession with Holly Willoughby would set him on a slow and steady path right back to prison and this time for much longer than his past infractions.

CHAPTER FOUR

Gavin Plumb by now had become an admin of a public Holly Willoughby fan group on a messaging app. Plumb was the moderator of the group - which gives you a good indication of what the conduct and discourse was like on the group. He used, among others, WhatsApp, Wickr *, and Kik. Kik Messenger is a free instant messaging app that allows users to send texts, images, and videos to each other from their smartphones. Launched in 2010, Kik gained popularity among younger users due to its anonymity and ease of use. The anonymity part was appealing to users like Plumb. The ability to chat in private groups too meant that like minded individuals were able to bring out the worst in one another and corrupt the more general purpose of this social technology.

That's the problem with the internet. There is no doorman to stop criminals and sex offenders from wandering in. The internet is the Wild West. The vast majority of people who use the internet are decent and ordinary. There are bad apples though who pollute this amazing communications technology. Gavin Plumb was one such bad apple. Kik was not a site favoured by hardcore criminals because it was possible for third parties (like the police) to access messages and groups. What made Kik appealing to men like Plumb is that it seemed to operate an anything goes policy with no moderation. You could literally talk about anything - however depraved or unpleasant.

Because the internet is still a relatively new technology it has been complex for the law to catch up. Most police forces tend to feel though, and it is hard to disagree, that you should not be allowed to say whatever you want on the internet. If someone was heard in public talking about abducting and raping someone than that person could rightly expect a visit from the police. Why should saying such things on the internet be any different? People have been busted for using Kik to share child abuse fantasies and photos. It wasn't Kik who uncovered this but third party involvement in the form of police. It is obviously impossible though for police forces to moderate the entire internet.

One of the problems police forces have faced is that dealing with these tech companies is a bureaucratic nightmare. They are notoriously difficult to get information out of. Anyone who has tried to contact one of these companies will probably have a story to tell about how difficult it was to find a human being to talk to and not get a vague meaningless response that wasn't computer generated. Or even a response at all - computer generated or not. Suffice to say, the customer service reputations of these types of companies is not brilliant. These sorts of companies have faced justified criticism and scrutiny regarding privacy and safety issues. The bottom line for these companies is profit and they sometimes give the impression that anything besides this is a nuisance they could happily live without.

The members (of whom there were about 50 to 100) of the Holly Willoughby group Plumb was in would discuss the celebrity object of their desire and share pictures. He had quickly graduated though from fairly innocent fan groups to more unpleasant ones. This was not surprising because Plumb was not really a fan of Holly Willoughby in the traditional sense of the word. He wasn't spending his online talking about what a good presenter or lovely fascinating person she was. He saw her merely as a fantasy sex object which he would love to seize and own. Plumb was therefore inevitably involved in a more private group where the members would discuss Holly Willoughby in more graphic and grim fashion. The profile picture that Plumb used for his account was one of Holly Willoughby in pyjamas which he'd found on the net.

The private fan group they'd set up had strict instructions that it was for 'Holly fans' only and no veering off topic would be tolerated. Gavin Plumb increasingly spent a lot of his time in this group sharing pictures of Willoughby taken from the net and talking about what he'd like to do to her. There were also some nude 'deep fakes' of Willoughby posted in the group - something which later became a criminal offence in Britain. The police later indicated that Plumb had been a member of many groups of this ilk and it was complex to retrieve all of his online activities. The criminal case against him in 2024 would mostly revolve around his activities on one specific group. It was on this group that Plumb would learn the hard way that people online are not always who they claim or appear to be.

Gavin Plumb was also a member of Google Plus and posted several messages about Willoughby there while it existed. Google Plus was a social networking platform developed by Google. Launched in June 2011, it was intended to compete with other social networks like Facebook and Twitter. Google Plus offered features such as Circles (for grouping contacts), Hangouts (for video chats), and a stream (similar to a news feed). Google Plus struggled to maintain engagement and failed to compete effectively with established social platforms. In October 2018, Google announced the shutdown of Google Plus for consumers, citing low usage and challenges in maintaining the service. The shutdown was completed in April 2019. Gavin Plumb was scoping out all of these places as he sought out online company and groups to talk about Holly Willoughby. He found a lot of these groups too tame for his liking though - which partly explains why he only did a handful of posts on Google Plus.

When it came to Holly Willoughby groups, Plumb didn't want what was on the shelves. He wanted the contraband under the counter version. Plumb's obsession with Holly Willoughby inevitably then led him into darker places which had no moderation, no filter, and no rules. With the username 'BigBear 341987', Plumb became a member of the 'Abduct Lovers' group - which, as the name suggests, was even grimmer yet than anything he'd previously participated in online. Abduct Lovers was a private group where members openly discussed the rape, kidnap and murder of female celebrities. The profile picture/logo for the group was of a frightened young woman with a male hand forcibly covering her mouth. Why are things like the Abduct Lovers group tolerated? This was a question that Essex Police would later raise.

Abduct Lovers catered to Plumb's darkest fantasies and put

him in touch with men who had the same thoughts and fantasies. Gavin Plumb had found his natural online home. He came to regard Abduct Lovers as his own private club. How many of these men were serious though? Was this mere online (sick) fantasy or were any of them actually ready to do these things? What about Gavin Plumb? Was he serious? Plumb would later strongly deny that he intended to do any of the things he talked about in the group. It was, said Plumb, all make believe. Merely online gratification and fantasy that would never bleed into the real world. That line of defence would inevitably be weakened though by Plumb's past criminal convictions. It is very difficult to maintain you would never dream of doing something when there is evidence that you have already done things which were very similar.

Gavin Plumb also had the more conventional social media pages like Facebook at this time. His Facebook book page was later retrieved and looked at by some news sites in the aftermath of his conviction in 2024 but it predictably didn't betray any hints or clues about his true nature or have any obvious red flags. Gavin Plumb was on his best behaviour on Facebook. He never mentioned Holly Willoughby at all on his Facebook page. This was not surprising really because Facebook was the 'public' face of Gavin Plumb and a place he used to keep in contact with family. The 'private' online Gavin Plumb of places like Abduct Lovers was a completely different person altogether.

The secret online Gavin Plumb was the same man who tried to abduct the women from the train or threatened those teenage girls with a knife at Woolworths. That was the real Gavin Plumb and in places like the Abduct Lovers group he no longer had to wear a mask or pretend to be anyone else. Though he would occasionally surface to do a 'normal' post on Facebook it was in the more disturbing depths of the net that Gavin Plumb increasingly spend most of his time. Plumb became addicted to this murky underbelly of the web where he could openly share his sickest and most sadistic fantasies. These online groups became a place where he could escape from his mundane dull life in the real world - a place where he'd known only rejection and disappointment.

Life had not dealt Gavin Plumb a very good hand of cards. He was overweight, bald, had blotchy skin, little education, minimal job prospects, and not much money. Of course he had not helped himself much either by getting a criminal record to boot. Gavin Plumb increasingly found reality to be a crushing disappointment and a place he didn't like very much. Plumb felt like reality was a place largely closed off to him. The online world was very different. All you needed was a computer and a username and you had unrestricted access. Plumb felt like a loser in the real world but it was different in places like Abduct Lovers where he found like minded people he could boast to about his crimes. Posing as a big cheese on Abduct Lovers appealed to Gavin Plumb. It was the one place where he felt important and respected. The fact that his audience was bedroom bound fantasists and sex criminals didn't bother him at all. These were 'his' people. He felt at home with them.

The dominant fantasy in Gavin Plumb's head was the thought of 'owning' Holly Willoughby and keeping her captive as his personal property. His very own Miranda Grey. Gavin Plumb became more and more obsessed with talking about his fantasy online and even started working out the logistics of how it might in theory be made to come true. Talking about this fantasy and immersing himself in its details was a lot more appealing than real life to Gavin Plumb. He seemed to think, or at least hope, if he posted endlessly about abducting Holly Willoughby in the grim and disturbing nooks and crannies of the internet he could somehow magically will this harrowing fantasy into existence.

As far as the actual logistics of abducting Holly Willoughby went, Gavin Plumb was always somewhat sketchy on the fine details. Plumb was not a criminal mastermind. He wasn't a professional kidnapper. This was a man so stupid he once tried to abduct two women on a train full of passengers. Was it the case though that the long gestation of this new abduction plan was because he had failed in the past? Was he determined not to make the same mistakes again? The fact that Plumb's new plan still didn't make much sense and was improbable at best was not something he seemed to be aware of. Plumb and his defence team in 2024 would try to use his lack of a coherent abduction plan to their advantage. They argued that the reason why Plumb's alleged plan to abduct Holly Willoughby didn't make an awful lot of sense is because it was never going to happen. It wasn't real so it didn't need to make sense or be realistic. It didn't matter if the plan was full of holes because it was just an online fantasy.

The prosecution would have an obvious counter to this though. They could simply point out that, given Plumb claimed it was just a fantasy, he certainly put a lot of time and thought into how one might abduct Holly Willoughby and even started purchasing items which might assist in an abduction. The prosecution didn't think the abduction was fanciful beyond belief. Their view was that Gavin Plumb had every intention of going through with this abduction and the only reason it didn't happen was because he was arrested. They conceded that Plumb wasn't the most intelligent person in the world and the plan may well have failed but they believed the intent was there and that Plumb would have attempted to kidnap and harm Holly Willoughby given the chance.

Plumb's obsession with Holly Willoughby went back way before his arrest and trial. He was discussing her online from 2014 at least and was aware of her long before this. In the end it was literally all he did with his time - go on the internet and talk about Holly Willoughby. And what he said about Holly Willoughby was beyond grim, menacing and full of threat.

The police also later established that Gavin Plumb had done web searches on things like 'how to meet people who want to abduct a celebrity'. If this was just, as Plumb later claimed, a harmless online fantasy why was he doing web searches like this? Plumb now spent the overwhelming majority of his time in the Abduct Lovers group sharing sexual fantasies about abducting Holly Willoughby.

Plumb would later tell the police the police that these were just meaningless private fantasies. Were it not for his previous criminal incidents and convictions it is possible that he might have been given the benefit of the doubt or a less stringent punishment at least. If his criminal slate was clean and he'd never committed any crimes against women or any crimes at all then the defence that Plumb was merely a bleak bedroom fantasist may have had a modicum of credibility. However, with two convictions for attempted kidnap (not to mention a couple of suspected rapes - which he was not charged with) involving four women on his CV one can see why a jury and the authorities decided not to take any chances with Gavin Plumb. A man capable of trying to restrain two sixteen year-old girls with tape at knifepoint is not someone you want to be affording the benefit of the doubt.

That was the obvious problem the defence team working on Plumb's behalf in 2024 faced at the trial. They could argue that the alleged planned abduction of Holly Willoughby was a preposterous notion but they couldn't argue that Plumb had never tried anything like this before because he had the criminal convictions to show for it. In the Abduct Lover's group, Gavin Plumb often discussed his plans with another member who had the username 'Marc'. Plumb got very friendly with Marc on the site and the pair exchanged hundreds of private messages and learned where one another lived. Plumb felt as if he'd found a kindred spirit in Marc and an online friend that he might soon meet in real life soon. The messages often indicated that Plumb was very eager for Marc to come to Essex to visit him.

Marc, like Gavin Plumb, seemed to spend most of his waking hours on this site swapping deep fake celebrity porn pictures and discussing which famous people he'd like to abduct and rape. They were two tragic peas in a rancid pod. These two made a grim duo but as sick as 'Marc' was even he paled in comparison to Plumb. Plumb (posting as BigBear) quickly became the dominant personality and 'leader' in this online group. He seemed more extreme and persistent than the others. His fantasies had more detail. If there was anyone in that group who seemed to think this talk was all real and they were really going to do this stuff it seemed to the bombastic user posting as BigBear. This awful online group gave Plumb a sense of importance and authority that he'd never found in the real world. So he began to slide deeper and deeper into this fake online world of weird synthetic friendships with equally dodgy and sick men. But was 'BigBear' merely a character he was playing or were BigBear's abduction plans and boasts things that Plumb really intended to do? Were they both one and the same?

The real identity of Gavin Plumb's online friend 'Marc' was 48 year-old Mark Mulligan from Dublin. As with Plumb, Mulligan had a bleak and disturbing criminal past in the real world. Mulligan was jailed in November 2014 for three and a half years after he admitted stalking a woman and also discussing raping her young son online. He also had a conviction for possessing and distributing child porn. This was the measure of the 'good friend' that Gavin Plumb had made online. These private chatrooms and groups were basically a haven for frustrated sex offenders or people who dearly wished they were sex offenders. It seems plausible to presume that, like Plumb and Mulligan, a good number of the members of this chat group had past convictions for sexual offences. It was wretched company to say the least. These men formed online friendships as they openly shared their violent and disturbing fantasies free from moderation or consequences. Or so they presumed.

Plumb seemed to be trying to recruit Mark Mulligan to help him in his Holly Willoughby abduction plans but Mulligan was partially deaf and couldn't drive. He wouldn't have been much use at all in the abduction plan that Plumb would never shut up about in this online group. Mulligan told Plumb that celebrities needed to 'be put in their ******* place'. Mulligan had a battery of Irish television and radio presenters who featured in his own twisted fantasies but Plumb didn't have too much interest in hearing about these Irish presenters because he'd never heard of any of them. He indulged Mulligan (or 'Marc') though because he felt he had made a good friendship here which deserved to be cultivated and cherished.

In addition to his private online activities, at this time Mulligan actually had a public profile on the (mainstream) dating site Plenty of Fish. He laughably described himself as a 'genuinely good person' in his profile. Among the hobbies he listed was 'visiting abandoned buildings'. Talk about sinister. You definitely wouldn't want to end up in an abandoned building with Mark Mulligan. Mulligan was a stark lesson in the dangers of the internet. You never quite know who you are really talking to sometimes. The 'genuinely good person' promised by the Plenty of Fish profile was in fact a convicted stalker who enjoyed child porn and discussing about which celebrities should be raped and killed.

On his dating website profile, Mulligan had written - "I'm easy-going, enjoy walking, photography. I go to the cinema now and then, enjoy when I can go to theatre, comedy gigs, watching few things on TV. I've taken up walking again as I want to lose a few pounds. If you want to know more feel free message me, I'm looking for a date and maybe possibly more depending on where the first date is going so no one night stand or anything." Mulligan was (no great surprise here) an odd character. In one of the few online pictures of him he's dressed as the cartoon character He-Man. Plumb shared this childlike quality in that he sometimes wore a Batman t-shirt and was said to collect Ghostbusters merchandise. He-Man and Ghostbusters were harmless and nice obsessions to have though. They were what you might describe as healthy geeky obsessions. Sadly, they came a very distant second to the less healthy obsessions that Plumb and Mulligan shared in the Abduct Lover's group.

The private messages flying back and forth between the new best pals Mulligan and Plumb soon became an endless flurry of activity. Mulligan greatly enjoyed talking about abductions online with 'BigBear'. In response to an especially vile flourish from Plumb in relation to Holly Willoughby, Mulligan said - 'One thing is guaranteed, Phil will need to get a new co-host.' It seems though that Mark Mulligan never had any genuine intention though of going to England to get involved in the abduction Plumb endlessly spoke about carrying out. Mulligan thought this online group was all about fantasies and had no desire to really take part in a crackpot scheme to abduct a famous television presenter in London. Though he enjoyed the fantasy and played along and although he was sadly all too capable of stalking Irish celebrities on his home turf, Mulligan must have been aware that Plumb was full of fanciful bluster. Mulligan knew that if they did try to go ahead with the Holly Willoughby abduction it was most likely to end in complete failure.

Plumb and Mulligan spent months discussing Holly Willoughby and increasingly shared fake explicit pictures of her. The most prized fakes for them were ones where female celebrities were tied up and restrained. Plumb told his new online friend that he didn't care about any 'consequences' that would come with kidnapping Willoughby. Plumb had no fear of the justice system in England. He had two convictions for sex offences and attempted kidnap but the mild sentences he got for these crimes had amounted to not much more than a slap on the wrist. Plumb had also been talking to another man online named Ryan (doubtless not his real name) who, according to Plumb, had expressed interest in participating in the abduction of Holly Willoughby. 'It might finally be happening,' an excited Plumb messaged Marc. Plumb also spoke to a member named 'Alfie Noakes' and said that he would be put on 'death row' for the things he wanted to do to Holly Willoughby.

Plumb liked to speak of his past criminal convictions to Marc and other online members as way to 'boost' his credibility and status in the group. Plumb was eager for his new 'friends' to know that he wasn't just all talk and had done these sorts of things for real - even if they hadn't gone quite so well as he might have hoped. Gavin Plumb truly loved this group. It had taken over his life. There he was, the big 'organiser', holding court on Abduct Lovers and acting as if kidnapping a major celebrity would be easy as shoplifting a packet of sweets from a shop. He loved the idea that he was putting a 'crew' of loyal like minded people together for a big abduction. In one of Plumb's messages to Marc, he said - 'Thought I'd give you an update, I've had a member of the Holly group reach out to me. He knows the location of an abandoned building and he's up for it big time. Erm he's gonna let me know when he can get time off work and then we're off mate. We're gonna go and do stakeout and bang job done, s***s going down as it stands. It might change cos he'll probably get cold feet.'

Plumb's defence team in court would argue he was just a sad online 'show off' who had got carried away with this fantasy to such an extent that he acted as if it was real in his online communications. They made it sound as if Plumb was like an over enthusiastic method actor in some amateur theatre production who had got too immersed in their role.

The prosecution took a very different view. Plumb was no actor according to them. The prosecution argued that Gavin Plumb and BigBear were one and the same. While Plumb's online posts about raping Holly Willoughby were grim enough, the most disturbing thing about his fantasies was how he also seemed to get off on talking about how he would have to murder the presenter once he was finished with her. Was he actually capable of this? Might he have killed those airline stewardesses if he had successfully abducted them?

The answer to this is that we simply don't know but it seems somewhat unlikely that Gavin Plumb was some potential serial killer given that he never attempted to kill anyone in his life. While a lot of killers begin their life of crime with sex offences (and then move to murder when this is no longer enough to satisfy them) there is no firm evidence that Plumb was ever on this deadly path. The truth is though that we simply don't know what Gavin Plumb would have done to Holly Willoughby or the previous women he had tried to abduct had he successfully held them captive. It doesn't seem beyond the realm of possibility that he would have used extreme violence leading to danger but it seems that sexual gratification was his primary motivation.

It is difficult to find any clear parallels in the case of Plumb and Holly Willoughby because he never stalked her or visited her home. He never actually met her in the end and was convicted for online threats. He did though send a private message to her Twitter once in a doomed attempt to make contact. He of course got no reply and Holly Willoughby most likely doesn't read random messages and emails to her official social media by strangers. She probably has staff to filter those things. Though the two cases were very different, Plumb seemed vaguely reminiscent of John Hinckley Jr in this respect - with Willoughby his version of Jodie Foster. John Hinckley Jr developed an unhealthy obsession with the (then) teenage actress Jodie Foster in the 1970s after she played an underage prostitute in the famous Martin Scorsese film Taxi Driver. Hinckley made repeated (and predictably unsuccessful) attempts to contact Foster and became so frustrated by his inability to make her take any notice of him that he decided to assassinate President Ronald Reagan in mimicry of the alienated vigilante Travis Bickle in Taxi Driver.

Hinckley, completely detached from reality, thought this murder would impress Foster and that the actress would finally notice him. Reagan survived the 1981 bullet and Hinckley was found not guilty by reason of insanity and remained under institutional psychiatric care until September 2016 (on July 27, 2016, a federal judge ruled that Hinckley would be allowed to be released as he was no longer considered a threat to himself or others - the pivotal conditions of his release are that he has no contact with the Reagan family or Jodie Foster or Foster's family or agent). Jodie Foster said the John Hinckley Jr incident put her off doing plays because she was too scared there might be some nutty obsessed fan in the front row. She has rarely talked about John Hinckley Jr because it was something she just wanted to forget. The victims of Plumb were of a similar mindset. They just wanted to forget all about him. It remains to be seen if Holly Willoughby will ever talk about the Gavin Plumb case and what it was like for her. That will obviously be entirely her decision.

It was established that Plumb had used Google Earth to research Holly Willoughby's location. He told 'Marc' that a lane running near her house might make a good place for an 'ambush'. He kept his options open though (Plumb's abduction plan changed so many it got confusing trying to make sense of it at times) and said he would buy masks for if they had to enter her house. 'Getting this bitch is all I can think about,' he messaged Marc. 'I've wanted this for years. I'm going to be living out my ultimate fantasy.' The prospect of this plan going wrong didn't bother Plumb too much. He told Marc that British prisons were no hardship because you could watch television in your cell and have your own phone. He made them sound like holiday camps. Plumb had now purchased a folding knife and was conducting research about chloroform and where one might obtain some online. This is where Gavin Plumb now resided. Lost in this delusional fantasy world where abducting Holly Willoughby was not a fantasy but something he could easily accomplish if he put his mind to it.

Holly Willoughby lived in a six bedroom $3 million Edwardian mansion overlooking the Thames in Barnes. She moved into this house with her family in 2012. Barnes, in a bend of the River Thames, is in the extreme north-east of Richmond upon Thames. Barnes was actually where the pop star Marc Bolan died in a car crash. It was also where the actor Robert Pattinson grew up. Because of its village atmosphere, elegant houses, and leafy aura, Barnes has traditionally been home to many celebrities down the years. Aside from Holly Willoughby, other current residents of Barnes include Ronan Keating, Gary Lineker, and the American actor Stanley Tucci. Holly Willoughby's house was walled off with a huge metal gate. In 2016, there were stories in the newspapers that Holly and her husband had wanted to add two new floors to the mansion but had their planning application rejected due to complaints by neighbours. The neighbours felt the changes would ruin the character of the street and they also didn't much like the idea of all the noise from builders and construction they would have to put up with for months as a consequence.

There were some tabloid stories that Holly Willoughby and her husband had annoyed the neighbours with noisy late night parties but Holly and her husband said these stories were not true. Having been foiled in their plan to build up there were then stories about the Willoughby's wanting to build down and making plans for a lavish 'super basement'. It wasn't exactly difficult to find some exterior photographs of Holly Willoughby's house online. Gavin Plumb certainly did this. The wall and gate was imposing but one side facing the road had a large hedge rather than simply a wall (though there was plainly something behind the hedge too). The hedge was less imposing than the gate and wall but it still stood much higher than a person. It was very difficult to imagine the lumbering Gavin Plumb getting over this hedge - at least not without breaking his neck. Even with a step-ladder it would have been a struggle for him and walking around South West London at night with a step-ladder would hardly have been inconspicuous would it?

Plumb's focus on abductions was alarming and weird but it seems that was his thing. This was the fantasy that gave him the biggest thrill. In the real world Holly Willoughby and most attractive women wouldn't give Gavin Plumb a second glance. Plumb was aware of this and this is why his abduction fantasies took root in his imagination and wouldn't go away. It was a method through which he could get what he couldn't ordinarily have. It was why Frederick Clegg abducted Miranda Grey. He knew Miranda Grey would be unattainable to him through conventional means so he came up with an unconventional (and criminal) solution. Plumb had gone down a similar path of twisted logic.

When the police later got access to Plumb's phone and devices they obtained access to thousands of his online conversations and a great many of them were read out at the trial. Needless to say, this was not very helpful at all when it came to Gavin Plumb's defence. When his online conversations were read out in court it didn't sound very much like a fantasy or a joke or make believe. He sounded like a man who was genuinely planning to abduct a celebrity and was seeking to recruit others to help him. Gavin Plumb, as you might expect, later begged to differ in court. He said this was all just an online fantasy that had got out of hand. He said he was embarrassed and ashamed by all the dreadful things he had said online but they were meant to be private.

The thing about Plumb's past abduction attempts on the train is that they displayed no thought or planning whatsoever. He just walked up to the women on the train with a plastic gun and told them to do as he said. Plumb had these disturbing and crazy desires that his impulses made him act on but beyond the actual 'moment' of approaching the woman he never had any idea what was going to happen next. This was most evident when he tried to restrain two co-workers in a Woolworths stockroom. How on earth had he expected to get away with that given he was at work and there were other staff nearby? It was as if Plumb was so fixated on the 'thrill' and excitement of the actual moment of attack that he never concerned himself with the aftermath. Plumb's crimes displayed hardly planning at all. That was the essential difference between his past crimes and his alleged scheme to abduct Holly Willoughby. This time you couldn't accuse Plumb of not putting any thought into the crime. It was literally all he did for months on end. Come up with ideas for a plan to kidnap Holly Willoughby.

Granted, a lot of the details were vague and nonsensical but the planning was there and the prosecution would later argue that the intention was there too. At one juncture during his online discussions in the Abduct Lover's group, Plumb had suggested that after the abduction he would keep Holly Willoughby captive in his own home as a temporary measure - which was clearly absurd. Plumb lived in a one-bedroom flat (with thin walls) on a housing estate. It was literally the worst place in the world to try and hide someone. How was he supposed to carry a struggling hostage into his flat without being seen by neighbours? What about all the CCTV cameras in the area? The thing is though that the idea was so appealing to Plumb - Holly Willoughby captive in his grotty bedroom - that the fine details didn't matter to him. And this is exactly what Plumb and his defence team argued in court. They argued that he was completely wrapped up in the fantasy but the actual plan was never a plan at all. He liked to talk about this stuff and think about this stuff but the plan was nonsense for the precise reason that Plumb never had any intention of acting on it.

Knowing that he was never going to do it, Plumb's defence team in 2024 argued that he never needed a working plan. The plan was a make believe fantasy plan. It didn't need to work because it was never going to be put to the test. The prosecution gave this explanation short shrift in court. They argued it was preposterous to think that a man who had two past convictions for attempted kidnap wasn't serious when he spoke of a kidnapping plan online. Plumb's increasingly dark and violent online posts about Holly Willoughby did not suggest a man happy to simply remain in the confines of fantasy.

There was a chilling blunt matter of factness about the way Plumb talked about the abduction online and in voice messages which made it sound very real. The prosecution pointedly noted this in court during the trial. The prosecution argued that if Plumb was simply 'getting off' on this abduction talk why was he so concerned with the boring practicalities of the plan? There was certainly though a lot of absurdity in Plumb's alleged Holly Willoughby kidnap plan. He talked at one point about how he was going to take a football along to the abduction because that way, if he was caught lurking in Holly Willoughby's garden by a police officer or neighbour (or perhaps even Mr Willoughby) he could just pretend he was simply retrieving his football after accidentally kicking it over the wall.

He had also though said the abduction (or 'home invasion' as Plumb liked to call it) would take place at night when no one was around. These two components of the plan did tend to clash in a way that would be obvious to anyone with a few brain cells. Was a police officer really going to believe a man in his late thirties was innocently having a football kickabout late at night and just by pure coincidence this happened to be right outside Holly Willoughby's house? Gavin Plumb would presumably have deduced all of this in the end had he actually gone ahead with the plan and made some modifications. Or maybe he wouldn't. Perhaps he really was that detached from reality.

At this point, Plumb had not yet discovered where exactly Holly Willoughby lived - although he did manage to find this information out in the end. He spoke online of researching her daily routine and said he only needed a 'rough idea' of where she lived and he'd find a place to 'strike' - though he felt a 'home invasion' would be much better than snatching her off the street. There is evidence that Plumb later discussed online an alley quite close to Willoughby's house which he identified as a good place to hide and gather in preparation for the abduction.

Alarmingly, Plumb was also found to have done web searches on Chay Bowskill. Chay Bowskill was the young creep and sociopath who forcibly kidnapped his former girlfriend Angel Lynn in 2020. Bowskill literally just ran up to Angel from behind while she was obliviously walking down a pavement, violently put her in a bear hug, and then quickly bundled her into a van where an accomplice was acting as the driver. The whole abduction only took seconds. After being snatched off the street by Chay Bowskill, Angel then fell from the vehicle at 60mph on the A6 in Leicestershire. She was left unable to walk or speak and required round the clock care - though she is thankfully showing some signs of improvement now.

Bowskill, who was a convicted thief and burglar and had been abusive and violent to Angel in the past, was sentenced to twelve years (he'd previously only been given seven years but this was reviewed and deemed too lenient) behind bars.

Given his research on the Chay Bowskill case, Plumb may have pondered how plausible it would be to bundle Holly Willoughby into a van from the street in similar fashion. It certainly sounded a lot easier than breaking into her house would be. The problem was though that Plumb did not own a van and did not drive. So he would need at least one accomplice of the type that Bowskill had somehow dragooned into helping him when he abducted Angel Lynn.

Plumb would also need detailed knowledge of Willoughby's routines and where she took walks near her home. The biggest obstacle to this course of action was that Holly Willoughby was a major celebrity in a well heeled part of South West London full of CCTV cameras. The chances of abducting Holly Willoughby in broad daylight and then getting very getting very far at all were fairly minimal you'd imagine. So, Gavin Plumb seemed to decide, a home invasion it was then. A street abduction was too risky. These frightening thoughts were all part and parcel of the bizarre and fantastical (not to mention disturbing) calculations which consumed most of Gavin Plumb's troubled headspace at this time. One can see then how the gulf between the defence and prosecution at the trial became a giant canyon of of polar opposites.

The prosecution asked the jury why Plumb was doing all of this elaborate online research and some plan revisions if the plan was merely fictional. It was certainly a difficult question for the defence to get around. All the defence at the 2024 trial could really say was look, it wasn't real, he got carried away online. The research, said the defence, was part of the 'fun' and 'gratification' for Plumb. That's all it was though according to the defence. Online games. He never made any attempt to stalk Willoughby and never visited her home. At one point Plumb claimed online that he had twelve men who were willing to assist in his abduction plan. He was probably exaggerating but he certainly discussed the plan in private with a fair few members. These men and potential accomplices all melted away in the end though. They liked talking about abducting celebrities but actually doing it was another thing altogether. Even if you are a sex offender and not exactly adverse to risk, if some person online you've never met asks you if you want to help him abduct Holly Willoughby you are not very likely to actually take him up on that.

There was evidence from the conversations between Plumb and Mulligan that Gavin Plumb seemed very interested in the Jill Dando case. In the 1990s, Jill Dando was one of the most recognisable and famous faces in Britain thanks to her duties as a newsreader for the BBC. Dando also hosted Crimewatch (a show which highlights unsolved crimes and appeals for fresh information) and the travel show Holiday. Jill Dando was literally all over the place. She was one of the most high profile presenters in the country and everyone knew who she was. On the morning of 26 April 1999, Dando was shot dead outside her home in Fulham. She was 37 years-old. The killer had shot her in the head and fled the scene. It was a shocking and baffling murder. Why on earth would anyone want to kill Jill Dando? That was to prove a question which rather perplexed the police.

After a huge police investigation (which naturally dominated the news headlines in Britain) into Jill Dando's the police arrested a local oddball named Barry George. George lived about a mile away from Dando. In 2001, Barry George was sentenced to life in prison for Jill Dando's murder but it was a conviction which troubled many because the evidence seemed far from conclusive. The police case against Barry George was dubious at best. They made great play of the fact that firearms residue had been found on his clothing but this was later proven to be so minuscule that it proved nothing. Half the population of London might be found to have a minuscule speck of firearms residue on them from brushing against someone on public transport.

The police also noted that Barry George had a few newspaper articles about Jill Dando in his flat. Given that George was a mentally troubled hoarder with about ten million newspapers in his flat it would have been impossible for none of these newspapers to mention Jill Dando because she was one of the most famous people in the country! Once again the police evidence proved nothing. The biggest problem with the police case against Barry George is that the murder was highly efficient. It was done very quickly and the killer was very elusive in escaping from the crime scene without detection. Barry George was a shambles of a man. It beggared belief to think that he would have been capable of this Mafia style assassination. George was clearly no angel. The police found evidence that he was something of a peeping Tom and sometimes followed women. There was no conclusive evidence that he was a murderer though. After three appeals, the conviction of Barry George was quashed in 2008 and he was set free. Jill Dando's killer has yet to be identified and the case remains unsolved.

We can only speculate on why Plumb was so interested in this case but perhaps it was because of the ease with which the assailant gained access to Dando. The killer simply walked up behind her as she was putting her key in the front door. This was actually a house that Dando didn't live in anymore and was selling. She was only there to collect some mail. Dando's home in Fulham was was much easier to approach though than Holly Willoughby's. Dando's house was close to the pavement and all you had to do was open the gate and you were virtually at her front door already. Willoughby's house was such that it was far less easy to just waltz up to the door. One interesting comparison in the cases is that it was impossible (despite police claims) to prove that Barry George had any particular interest in Jill Dando. There were no pictures of her on the wall in his flat. There was no Jill Dando scrapbook. No videos of her taped off the television. No pictures of her cut out of newspapers. There was though a shrine in the flat to Freddie Mercury.

The police said that George was found to have four copies of the BBC in-house magazine Ariel memorial to Jill Dando in his flat but it's hard to see how this evidence could be used against him. Many people kept newspaper memorials after the death of Princess Diana but it doesn't mean they killed her! Besides, Barry George used to work as a runner at the BBC and it was there (years before Dando was famous) that he started collecting Ariel magazine. In contrast to Barry George and Jill Dando, the police and prosecution had ample evidence that Plumb was obsessed with Holly Willoughby. On this front they had evidence coming out of their ears. Plumb had thousands of pictures of Holly Willoughby on his computer. His online communications and phone texts revolved around Willoughby for nearly two years leading up to his arrest. It seemed as if, for months on end, Holly Willoughby was the only thing on Gavin Plumb's mind.

Plumb's voice mails discussing the abduction plan were chilling for the calm mundane way he talks about the plans. At one point he suggests abducting two celebrities one after the other. An unnamed celebrity (only referred to as 'Lucy') who another Abduct Lover's member wanted to kidnap and then Holly Willoughby. Plumb discusses selecting these celebrities much like a man pondering what to order from a Chinese takeaway menu. The unreality of Plumb's state of mind was betrayed not just by the grim and violent flourishes but also by the strange small details. Plumb at one point mentions buying some new handkerchiefs for Holly Willoughby to use while she is temporally stashed in his flat. Plumb acts as if this is an incredible act of kindness she'll be eternally grateful to him for. If you've been abducted by some rapist lunatic it is probably safe to presume that having some fresh hankies to use isn't going to mitigate the fear and distress very much.

Plumb's digital trail of misogyny and hateful and violent sexual threats (towards an actual real person) in the awful chat group was extensive and disgusting. He was literally the worst person in this group when it came to content and contributions and that was really saying something given the miserable company he was keeping. Gavin Plumb had become addicted to this private chat group. He believed he had made real friends there - which was a delusion because none of these men wanted to meet Plumb in real life. He seemed to believe that someone somewhere in the group would be able make his abduction fantasies become real choices and options. All he needed to do was find that person.

Plumb loved holding court as 'BigBear' and letting all his darkest desires roam free onto this little squalid corner of the net. He enjoyed messaging people and sharing new details he'd picked up about the life of Holly Willoughby. Plumb was so comfortable in this group by now he almost had a sense of ownership as if it was his own private space. What he didn't realise was that the private chat group had lulled him into a false sense of security. He thought all of this was private talk between like minded people which never went beyond the walls of Abduct Lovers. Much to the shock and surprise of Gavin Plumb though, that didn't actually quite turn out to be the case at all.

* Wickr is a messaging app that provides secure and private communication for its users. It enables end-to-end encryption for messages, voice calls, video calls, and file sharing, ensuring that only the intended recipients can access the content. Wickr emphasises privacy and security, allowing users to send messages that can be set to self-destruct after a certain period. This makes it appealing for individuals and organisations that prioritise confidentiality. The app has features like encrypted group chats, support for various media types, and the ability to communicate without

requiring a phone number. Wickr is commonly used in environments where privacy is crucial, such as by journalists, activists, and businesses dealing with sensitive information. Of course, these features are sadly also attractive to criminals, sex offenders, and predators.

CHAPTER FIVE

Unknown to the unsuspecting Gavin Plumb and the other 'members', the Abduct Lovers group (which had members from around the world and not just in Britain) had been infiltrated by an undercover police officer from the Owatonna Police Department in Minnesota in the United States. This was the 3rd of October, 2023. The police officer, who obviously has his real identity protected, started posting on the group with the username David Nelson. He was part of a cyber surveillance team operating from his police station. The police officer's duties involved investigating the murky dark toilets of the online world to identify any potential dangers. His job was to try and prevent or uncover murders, rapes, human trafficking, and kidnappings by criminals who liked to go to secret places online to talk about their crimes and things they planned to do. If you were a police officer engaged in such cyber duties then a group called Abduct Lovers with a frightened woman as its logo was obviously going to pique your interest and make you feel duty bound to investigate. And so this is exactly what the police officer (who would later give his evidence anonymously at Plumb's trial) did.

The arrival of 'David Nelson' into the group was very bad news for the unwitting Gavin Plumb - who was still, as usual, engaged in talking about his plan to abduct Holly Willoughby to anyone who would listen. Police forces are now very active in this sort of online undercover work. In online police work in Britain alone, thousands of people are arrested each year for attempting to groom children online and sending them explicit pictures. Police officers will often pose as underage girls or boys online to expose these predators. The American police officer on the Abduct Lover's group was doing something slightly different in that he was seeking to establish if any of the members of the Abduct Lovers group were genuinely violent and dangerous in the real world. He had to judge if any of these men were deadly serious and planned to meet the celebrities they talked about in such harrowing and worrying terms.

The American police officer had been doing this undercover online work for three years now so had built up a good amount of experience. The most important part of his work was managing to cement himself within these dark web style or private groups without attracting any suspicion. He basically had to convincingly pretend to be a sicko like the other men in these groups. He had to gain the trust of the other members and then try to isolate and get more information on anyone that struck him as a credible danger not confined to online fantasy. The police officer Nelson (to use his fake name) quickly seemed to zero in on Gavin Plumb among the members of the Abduct Lovers group. The user posting as 'BigBear' was a big giant red flag to Nelson and triggered all manner of alarm bells so the police officer decided to had to know more about this man. He would have to cultivate an online friendship with BigBear and talk to him.

All of Plumb's considerable efforts to establish himself as the 'big character' in this group were about to disastrously rebound on him in spectacular fashion and shatter his life. And it would all occur rapidly in a mere matter of hours. BigBear's posts, Nelson felt, went well 'beyond' the stuff posted by others on the Abduct Lovers group. Plumb seemed to be the most extreme person there. There was something about Plumb's posts which didn't sound like make believe. It didn't seem like a game to him. So it was 'BigBear' who the police officer became drawn to in the group. Given that Nelson's job was to prevent crimes from happening he obviously tended to work on the theory that it is much better to be safe than sorry. He had a duty to find out as much about Plumb as he could in as short a time as possible.

The police officer began responding to Plumb in the group and Plumb took the bait. The pair were soon engaged in conversations through private messaging. In his private messaging with Plumb, Nelson pretended his real name was Cameron Anderson and also pretended he was in New York. Neither of these things were true but it was a way to gain trust and therefore have 'BigBear' reciprocate by revealing his real name and location. The police officer was obviously not alone when he did this work because he was in a busy police station. Other police officers in the station engaged in this sort of cyber investigation work looked at the posts he'd found in the group and also his private messaging with 'BigBear' and agreed with him that Plumb seemed potentially dangerous and worthy of more online investigation.

When he first began investigating the group, Nelson noticed that 'BigBear' seemed to be talking about and posting a lot of pictures of a blonde haired woman who, being from the United States, he didn't recognise at all. Plumb was also endlessly talking about this blonde haired woman and how he wanted to abduct her. The undercover police officer asked Plumb who the blonde 'hottie' was and Plumb told him this was Holly Willoughby. He explained to Nelson that Willoughby was a famous television personality in Britain. In their private messaging, Plumb then told Nelson he had a lot of 'info' about Holly Willoughby. Where she lived, her daily movements and routine, CCTV at her house, what security she did or didn't have. Because he had a SIA (Security Industry Authority) licence, which is basically just a legal requirement for anyone who has ever worked in security, Gavin Plumb liked to think of himself as something of an expert in this field. A short stint working as a security guard was about the extent of his experience though. He wasn't exactly Jason Bourne.

Gavin Plumb, plainly desperate to find anyone in the group willing to listen to his incessant and vile Holly Willoughby abduction ideas, was delighted to have found this American online who seemed to share his abduction fantasies and asked him many questions about his favourite subject Holly Willoughby. Nelson had now suddenly supplanted 'Marc' as Plumb's main online friend in the group. Nelson, despite the fact that he lived across the Atlantic thousands of miles away, sounded to Plumb like an altogether more promising and useful potential accomplice than Marc. Gavin Plumb obviously had no idea that he was now talking to a police officer online because he divulged a lot of information - information that would soon to be used to locate, identify and arrest him.

The clandestine nature of sites like Abduct Lovers had given Plumb a false sense of security. He thought everyone there was just like him. The notion that undercover police officers lurked in these places from some high tech police office thousands of miles away was not something that had crossed Plumb's mind. Plumb told Nelson that he intended to stage a home invasion on Holly Willoughby. Home invasion is a common term for a subgenre of horror films - which may have been where Plumb got this term from. We've all seen umpteen horror films where people are besieged in their home. 'We break in when they are in bed,' messaged Plumb, 'we hold both at a weapon point, tell both to roll over on there [sic] fronts with there [sic] hands behind their backs. With Dan (Holly Willoughby's husband) we use the metal cable ties, with Holly we'll use the handcuffs etc...'

Plumb relished having someone new to listen to his abduction ideas. The private messages between Plumb and his new American 'friend' quickly escalated into the dozens and then into the hundreds. Plumb said that chloroform would be used on Holly Willoughby and her husband and she would be taken to a remote location where her screams would not be heard for miles (this was a line that Marc had previously said to him). Plumb was clearly getting off on writing this stuff but was he really planning to do it? David Nelson (to use his fake username again) decided there might be a legitimate threat to Holly Willoughby from this rather disturbing man he was talking to online. So he decided to keep Plumb talking in an attempt to gather more information and deduce how serious and how imminent this threat to Willoughby might potentially be.

Plumb told Nelson that Holly Willoughby would be raped and then eventually her throat would be slit. He would 'clean her out with bleach' (whatever that meant) and then dump the body in a lake (of which there were quite a few in Essex where Plumb lived). Gavin Plumb said to more than one online member of Abduct Lovers that they would also make Holly Willoughby record a video message in which she said she had gone away of her own free will. Plumb said this would 'clear' them of any criminality because Holly would have agreed to all of this. That last statement was clearly preposterous. It would be like saying someone in a hostage video doesn't need to be rescued or the kidnappers pursued because they must have happily agreed to be kidnapped!

These sorts of bewildering and plainly stupid details were what Plumb's defence team tried to pick up on in court in 2024. His barrister insisted that his abduction plan was so stupid and so fantastical that it couldn't possibly be taken seriously as if it was something Gavin Plumb was actually going to carry out. The subtext of his defence team was obvious. Yes, Gavin Plumb posted some sick stuff online. He had some truly awful fantasies. But he's not THAT stupid. He wasn't actually going to do this stuff in real life. The American police officer and the prosecution took a very different point of view on this whole grim affair. They felt Gavin Plumb was so obsessed with Holly Willoughby that he posed a genuine threat to the television presenter. They felt it was very plausible to think that Plumb would have gone ahead with his online plans. They argued in court that the only reason why the abduction didn't go ahead is because it was interrupted and stopped before it could happen.

Gavin Plumb told Nelson that Holly Willoughby's car could be used as the getaway vehicle once the home invasion of her house had taken place. Once she was incapacitated they could break into her car and escape - racing off into the South West London night with Holly Willoughby in the boot. Plumb did not have a driving licence but he had been taking driving lessons - only a few though at the time. Suffice to say, this plan was not exactly airtight when it came to logic or details. Plumb sounded like a man who had watched too many films. The notion that he could get over the wall, break into the house, incapacitate the husband, abduct Holly Willoughby and THEN escape in her own car ALL at night without attracting the attention of neighbours or the police or setting off numerous alarms was patently ridiculous. The area where Holly Willoughby lived was chock full of CCTV cameras. Her car would be identified very quickly. Gavin Plumb's fantasies seem to extend into thinking he was Jason Statham in the Transporter films.

Plumb was hardly likely to be capable of speeding out of London swiftly on the back of a couple of driving lessons and he still hadn't found an accomplice who could drive. The prosecution would argue though is that this was what made 'David Nelson' appealing to Gavin Plumb. Plumb, they argued, seemed to think he had finally found a competent accomplice who wasn't wasting his time. Plumb saw Nelson as someone who could act as the accomplice and perhaps the driver too. Of course, an American would know next to nothing about the geography of South West London and need detailed directions from Plumb. Would Plumb be capable of providing these precise directions?

This was the crux of the debate over Plumb's abduction case. The defence argued that when you placed Gavin Plumb's abduction plan under even the slightest scrutiny it fell apart very quickly. They argued that the plan wasn't credible and never reached a point where it was ready to go into action. The point of the defence was that Plumb spent about two years endlessly talking about this abduction online but never actually tried to carry it out. The defence believed that Plumb enjoyed talking about this abduction online much more than he relished the thought of actually trying to go through with it. They sought to persuade the jury that the abduction plan was an illusion. A fantasy that Gavin Plumb loved talking about but knew he could never actually try for real.

Most of the people Plumb spoke to online decided (sensibly) they didn't want to get involved in his Holly Willoughby abduction plan. They liked to go along with the fantasy for a while (for this was ostensibly the whole point of the Abduct Lovers group in the first place) but then drifted off one by one when they sensed that Plumb seemed more serious and persistent about his specific fantasy than other members were about their own ones. There were a number of other members in the group who Plumb messaged with for a time before regular contact was broken and they then seemed to then avoid him. A frustrated Plumb actually told one of them he would do the abduction on his own if he had to - which was plainly a hollow boast. If he'd been on his own, Plumb probably wouldn't even have got over the wall or in the house let alone kidnapped Holly Willoughby.

Plumb spoke online of putting together a crack 'crew' for the abduction attempt as if he was some gangland boss planning a big heist. No one was genuinely interested in helping or meeting him though and this is what made David Nelson interesting to Plumb and someone he quickly latched onto in the group. Nelson was convincing enough to make

Plumb feel as if - at long last - he had found someone who really was willing to help and might actually have experience of this sort of stuff (that is to say abducting people) before. A number of people in the Abduct Lovers group actually blocked Gavin Plumb in the end because they got fed up being pestered by this man wanting them to help him kidnap Holly Willoughby. They seemed to mostly know this was all a game.

The question of whether Gavin Plumb knew this was all pretend was more complex. He seemed to think a chat group for sickos was some sort of mystical place where fantasies could come true. The people he was talking to were not master criminals and experienced kidnappers though. They were largely bored fantasists and sex offenders who rarely left the house. At one point during their private communications, Plumb even told David Nelson he had someone to 'practice' on and sent a photograph of a female neighbour whom he'd evidently been collecting secret pictures of. One can see that the young mother was right to complain about Plumb setting up CCTV cameras which would pick up footage of his neighbours coming and going.

One of the most bizarre posts by Plumb was when he even suggested to Nelson his teenage son might take part in the abduction too. Plumb was estranged from the mother of his children but in court it was reported that his son (who was fifteen years-old in 2023) occasionally visited Gavin Plumb's flat. There was no truth though to Plumb's claim that his son might take part. It was just something he made up. Gavin Plumb clearly liked having a chat group like this where there were no rules and no filter. He just posted any crazy sick stuff that came into his head. David Nelson tested Plumb by asking for more information and proof of intent where the abduction was concerned. In response, Plumb sent him a short video in which he shot in his flat (from a first person perspective) and displayed the restraint kit he planned to use on Holly Willoughby.

Nelson would later tell the court at the trial that Plumb also shared information with him on where Willoughby lived. Around this time, Plumb had got a job as a security guard at a business park in Harlow (which was remarkable when you think about it, a two-time convicted sex offender working as a security guard). He spoke online of booking some days off so that he could put his kidnap plan into action. It later transpired in court that Abduct Lovers was not the only online group discussing rape and kidnap which Plumb was a member of. Plumb spent a lot of time searching for private groups like this to post on. He was on some other groups with the username 'Bear Master'.

The American police officer had to strike a delicate balance in his online dealings with Gavin Plumb because if it transpired that he used the David Nelson 'character' to coerce or entrap or encourage Plumb into a crime or talking about a crime this would obviously weaken any potential trial. The police officer had to allow Plumb to make decisions and responses of his own free will. As we have noted, Gavin Plumb spoke online about his past crimes more than once. Plumb lamented the fact that his 'tactics' in the Woolworths attack hadn't been very logical. 'If I'd planned it,' messaged Plumb, 'I would have got them into the smaller storage room that only had one exit and entrance, and was soundproof.' Plumb also spoke of his attempted train abductions online and seemed to regret the lack of planning and thought that had gone into them.

Plumb clearly relished the chance to talk about this stuff. It seemed to irritate him that he had not taken taken full advantage of these past situations where he had frightened women briefly under his control. One thing Plumb's private messaging completely contradicted was his spurious claim that he had only done these things to get arrested and wasn't going to harm or molest these women. Because this was a private chat group and Plumb always thought he was talking to a like minded person, he was honest about these past criminal incidents. He seemed proud of having done these things with no hint of shame. His only regret was that they hadn't been more successful.

In his online chats, Plumb referred to the air stewardesses he had threatened on the train as 'slags'. The fact that the women in question were greatly frightened and affected by these incidents and struggled to get over them was not something that ever occurred to Plumb. Sex criminals never consider the victims of their crimes. They only care about their desires. David Nelson asked Plumb if he wanted some help in his abduction plan and offered to fly from New York (where he was pretending to be based) to England. He wanted to know if Plumb was serious first though. Plumb assured Nelson that he was serious about the abduction of Holly Willoughby. Nelson even took the step of sending Plumb a picture of an airline ticket he had purchased just to gauge how Plumb responded to the thought of someone actually agreeing to help him and flying over to meet him.

Plumb wasn't phased by this and did not back down or make excuses. He insisted he was still serious. Plumb even sent Nelson (or Cameron Anderson as he was in private chat) a photograph of himself to prove he was a real person. Plumb now seemed to be under the impression that Nelson was some veteran sex criminal, professional kidnapper or hitman. He would later deny this in court, saying he developed some doubts about Nelson which made him suspicious. Even if this was true it was too late anyway. Plumb had said more than enough to incriminate himself. Plumb's claim of doubting the veracity of Nelson was not evident in their online communications. They even agreed a secret code word to use as a reference to the abduction. The code word was 'Holly'. 'S***, it's really happening,' messaged Plumb when he was sent evidence of the airplane ticket.

CHAPTER SIX

On October the 4th 2023, the police officer who had been posting as David Nelson on the Abduct Lovers group and private messaging with Plumb, held a meeting with the FBI and discussed Gavin Plumb. The police officer had talked to Plumb online over the course of 30 hours and in that time they had exchanged around 300 private messages. The information the officer had collected indicated, in his professional opinion, that Plumb was an imminent threat to Holly Willoughby (who the FBI had doubtless never heard of until the police officer turned up). The decision was made to send this information to the authorities in Britain and so this information was passed onto the National Crime Agency - who in turn passed this information to the Met Police in London and also the Essex Police.

As this was all going on, Gavin Plumb was in his Essex flat discussing Holly Willoughby online, playing a few video games, drinking tea, and going about his usual routines. If someone had told him then and there he was currently the subject of an FBI conference call thousands of miles away in a foreign country he probably wouldn't have believed it. Gavin Plumb wasn't the first person who seemed to be unaware that you can attract the attention of the police for things you say online and he won't be the last person either.

It probably wasn't a call the Essex Police were expecting that day. They were going about their usual business investigating local crimes and then suddenly there was this bizarre bolt out of the blue. A warning from the FBI that a local man from Harlow was about to kidnap Holly Willoughby!

They had no option but to take this high level tip-off seriously. This was presumably then heightened when they deduced from their records that Plumb had a criminal record for trying to abduct two women on a train and trying to restrain two female co-workers in a Woolworths store. A police team was quickly assembled for a raid on Plumb's flat. They arrived at his home at about 9-45 pm. The unsuspecting Gavin Plumb was about to get a very big surprise. For all his endless talk about staging a home invasion on Holly Willoughby, well, Plumb was about to experience a special home invasion himself. Gavin Plumb was shirtless when he was surprised in his flat. The lights were off and he was on the phone when the police smashed in his door (which seemed a bit over the top) with a battering ram. "What the hell is going on?" a completely bemused Gavin Plumb asked the police officers rushing in to arrest him.

One of the police officers had the presence of mind to immediately snatch Plumb's phone from him. This was shrewd because it gave them access to what he had been engaged in at the precise moment that they smashed his door in. Plumb was actually on one of the Holly Willoughby groups when the police arrived. A quick glance at his phone confirmed that this was the right man. This was the Holly Willoughby obsessed dangerman the FBI had tipped them off about through undercover police work conducted in the United States. When he was told he was being arrested on suspicion of conspiracy to kidnap, a still bewildered and confused Plumb replied by saying "What the hell are you talking about?"

At this point the penny had not yet dropped for Gavin Plumb that his online activities had prompted this late visit from the police. He asked who it was he was supposed to be planning to kidnap. He was told this would be explained to him at the police station but then a female police officer eventually told him it was Holly Willoughby. There was a detectable hint of disbelief in the police officer's voice as she said this. It was if she could hardly believe this strange arrest was actually real and happening. The bewildered response of Plumb when the police entered his flat was genuine initially. He was shocked and surprised. He had no idea what was going on. Plumb must have initially thought that perhaps they had the wrong flat and the police were staging a drugs raid on a neighbour or something.

However, this confusion on his part began to clear when the police mentioned the kidnap plan. The wheels in Plumb's mind slowly turned over and then finally deduced what this was really about. It must have dawned on Plumb quite quickly that all his vile online activity, all of his talk of abducting Holly Willoughby, had somehow come to the attention of the police. When the police mentioned Holly Willoughby one could see Plumb visibly start to deflate. "Okay," he said weakly. He now knew exactly what was going on now. All of those months he'd spent online talking about Holly Willoughby in the most ghastly way, the thousands of grim private messages about abduction, rape, and murder. All of this had come back to haunt him. He was now in very big trouble.

Gavin Plumb admitted that Holly Willoughby was a 'fantasy' of his but denied the charges that he was planning to kidnap and harm her. He said Holly Willoughby was a fantasy of many people. While that might have had some grain of truth, other people with a celebrity crush on Holly Willoughby didn't spend every waking hour on the internet talking about abducting and raping her and make plans for this abduction to such a realistic extent they start sending off for metal cable ties and chloroform. Asked for his phone pin code by the police, Plumb said "Nah, you don't need that now." As you might imagine, he was certainly not too eager for the police to start examining his phone and computer history.

The police said that trawling through Plumb's messaging and internet history was very complex because he had so many devices. Despite the fact he was often unemployed, Gavin Plumb's flat was festooned with the latest computer equipment. He had an X-Box, PlayStation, multiple laptops, the latest phones, and more besides. Where did he get all the money from? In the end, not all of Plumb's online activity and communications were retrieved but what the police did manage to extract was still considerable and highly disturbing and threatening. Gavin Plumb would later argue that 'online talk' is just talk and meaningless. The police pointed out though if one were to threaten to abduct, rape, and kill someone in public conversation that would not be tolerated and you would be arrested if this was reported. Why should the internet be any different?

The things that Plumb said online would not be acceptable in the real world but the groups he posted on and the online company he kept had 'normalised' this talk and behaviour to the point where it wasn't a big deal to Gavin Plumb and the others. But we know from his background that, deep down, Plumb was like this in real life too. If he saw an attractive woman his thoughts quickly turned to how much he'd like to abduct her and rape her. That was the way his mind worked. Were it not for his well documented weight problems (where he literally couldn't get out the flat and could barely stand up) he most likely would have landed back in prison again long before 2023. If he'd been fit and mobile it is hard to imagine Plumb wouldn't have tried to abduct another woman long before the Holly Willoughby case.

All of his disgusting online activity in relation to Holly Willoughby, all of his talk about planning to kidnap her and keep her prisoner as a sex slave, well, that had all now rebounded on Gavin Plumb. More than that, it now threatened his freedom. Plumb had experienced a terrifying bombshell. The sudden realisation that all the stuff he had said about Holly Willoughby was not private. It was being monitored in the end by the American police and now the Essex Police knew about it too. The danger of groups like Abduct Lovers is that the men posting there felt no sense of shame because they were in a community that shared their thoughts and desires. So the abduction and rape talk became something that didn't feel strange or forbidden to them. It became normal.

As some experts pointed out, the biggest danger of these types of groups is that the online fantasy isn't enough for some of these men. In fact, talking about the fantasy ultimately makes some of the men more determined to do something like this for real and we know that Gavin Plumb had attempted similar for real twice in the past. Gavin Plumb was clearly never just content with the fantasy. He never dropped the online fantasy abduction chat group addiction and moved onto something else - something more normal or healthy. He stuck doggedly to his Holly Willoughby abduction obsession as if it was the only thing in the world that he truly cared about. The police had no option but to take Gavin Plumb seriously and investigate him.

Once he'd composed himself, Gavin Plumb berated the police officers for smashing his door in with a battering ram. He told them all they had to do was knock and he'd have let them in. It was a reasonable complaint because smashing the door in did seem a trifle dramatic. It isn't as if Plumb (still a hefty and clumsy lump of a man despite the weight loss) was going to jump over the balcony like Spider-Man and sprint to freedom. The police said they smashed the door in because they didn't want him to have the chance to destroy evidence. Plumb didn't even know why they were here though initially so presumably would have answered the door anyway. Even if he'd known why they were here it is hard to see how he could have destroyed the evidence in a matter of seconds. It isn't as if he was going to flush hard drives and phones down the toilet and, besides, a lot of the digital evidence resided in the Owatonna Police Department in Minnesota thousands of miles away.

The police later released some footage of Gavin Plumb in custody in the station immediately after the arrest. Given the circumstances he seemed remarkably relaxed as he sat with his arms folded in a green t-shirt. He smirked and smiled and wasn't intimidated by the situation at all. Plumb struck one as a confident personality in the footage - which was certainly counter to the man who appeared in the BBC film about obesity. Perhaps it was the case that losing some weight had given Plumb more confidence. Or maybe that was the real Gavin Plumb with or without the weight. A cocky man full of bluster who thought he could get away with anything.

At this stage Plumb didn't seem too concerned by the strange predicament he had found himself in. He seemed to think that the idea of being convicted or banged up for saying some distasteful things about Holly Willoughby online was not especially credible. Plumb must have been aware though that the situation was very serious. The police were clearly not taking his Holly Willoughby abduction talk on the internet lightly at all. They had smashed his door in and arrested him late at night. Under legal advice, Plumb clammed up and refused to answer any questions. The Essex Police released a statement which read - "A 36-year-old man from Harlow has been arrested on suspicion of conspiracy to kidnap as part of an ongoing investigation. The arrest was made on Wednesday 4th October. He is currently in custody." Plumb appeared at Chelmsford Magistrates Court on 6 October, where he was remanded into custody on charges of soliciting to commit murder and incitement to kidnap, rape, and murder.

Holly Willoughby had been informed of the abduction plot the day before Plumb was arrested and given police protection. At this time her connection to this arrest was not in the public sphere. The day that Plumb appeared in court, Holly Willoughby was absent from her presenting role on This Morning. Willoughby was absent for the rest of the week and then announced her departure from the show. "It's been an honour to just be part of its story and I know this story has many chapters left to go," said Willoughby in a statement. "Sadly, however, I now feel I have to make this decision for me and my family." The Gavin Plumb connection quickly became public and Holly Willoughby's abrupt exit from This Morning suddenly made sense and was perfectly understandable. To be told by the police that someone was apparently plotting to abduct and murder her must have been very frightening.

Holly Willoughby was not the first This Morning presenter to experience trouble thanks to an obsessed fan. A man named James Haviland was convicted for spending two years stalking Willoughby's predecessor Fern Britton. James Haviland constantly sent Britton flowers and notes and even rented a cottage she owned in Cornwall close to her home just so he could be near her. When she found out the renter of the cottage near her home had the same name as the person sending her cards and flowers, Britton contacted the police. It transpired that James Haviland set up a stool upstairs in the cottage so he could see directly into Fern Britton's garden. Haviland was handed a restraining order for ten years, banning him from entering Cornwall. He was also banned from contacting Fern Britton. In her victim statement, Britton said - "It is worrying me; I would like him to stop before he does more. There is a point where you know it is inappropriate and I'm asking myself what his endgame is here? I am entitled to live a life that is pleasant, enjoyable and free of worry."

A jury in court would now have to decide how real Gavin Plumb's online abduction plot really was but all Holly Willoughby knew at the time was that some crazy fan was apparently planning to kidnap her. In November 2023, Plumb appeared in a pre-trial and plea hearing at Chelmsford Crown Court. Plumb confirmed his name and address and entered a not guilty plea to the charges of soliciting to commit murder and incitement to kidnap. Later in the month his bail application was refused. Detective Superintendent Rob Kirby, of Essex Police, said: "This was an extremely fast-paced investigation, with many of our officers and national partners working overnight to secure these charges. The safeguarding of any victim is paramount and we will continue to prioritise this and working with the Metropolitan Police Service as the investigation proceeds." The trial was set for June the following year.

Detectives examining Plumb's phone and computer devices discovered 10,322 images of Holly Willoughby. He had also shared 'deep fake' pornographic pictures of Willoughby online. Plumb plainly had an all consuming Holly Willoughby obsession. It what was a laborious but necessary task, the police had to establish if all of these pictures came from the net. They had to make sure that Gavin Plumb hadn't got close enough to Holly Willoughby to take a real photograph. That is to say, they had to establish if Plumb had been stalking Holly Willoughby and visited the streets near where she lived. It turned out though that all of his pictures of Holly Willoughby came from the net. They were pictures that (apart from the deep fake porn pictures) anyone could find through a normal image search.

It was established then that Gavin Plumb never visited Holly Willoughby's house to scope it out. He never tried to follow her and he never visited the ITV studios where she had worked (though he did mention online that he'd like to visit the This Morning studios). While this did not mean he was off the hook, the fact that he had never gone anywhere near Holly Willoughby in real life was at least a tiny crumb for any legal defence of Gavin Plumb. It meant the defence could adopt a strategy of claiming this was simply a pathetic online fantasy that never went any further than Plumb's grubby keyboard.

During his private online conversations with 'David Nelson', Plumb had talked at one point about getting his son involved in the Holly Willoughby abduction. The police had to speak to Plumb's son to see if there was any truth in this. It transpired though that this was simply something Plumb said online as a weird sort of boast or suggestion. In reality, Plumb had minimal contact with his son and Plumb's son was just a normal teenager happily getting on with his life. He obviously had no idea that his largely estranged father spent most of his time trawling the more unpleasant chat groups on the web and talking about kidnapping and raping Holly Willoughby.

Of particular interest to the police was not just the information collected by the American police officer but also Plumb's online conversations with 'Marc' - which became an important component of the case against him. Marc had certainly seemed enthusiastic at times discussing the abduction plan with Plumb but it often appeared he enjoyed the fantasy and chat more he actually liked the prospect of actually attempting this for real. There are several occasions in the conversations between Plumb and Mulligan where 'Marc' seems on the cusp of actively participating (even going so far as to ask for directions to where Plumb lives) or pretending to want to get involved but then comes up with a convenient excuse as to why he can't.

Marc says at one point that Covid restrictions make it hard for him to leave Ireland. On another occasion he tells Plumb he's just been arrested and so can't leave home. And so on. Plumb enjoyed talking to Marc about the abduction but in the end seemed to sense that Marc was not actually going to help him do this thing - the thing which Plumb claimed was just a fantasy. The police managed to retrieve most of Plumb's communications with Marc and they formed the backbone of the case against him. When you added Plumb's online posts and communications with the undercover police officer and other Abduct Lovers users, well, this all tallied up to a huge amount of material and evidence which did not bode well for Gavin Plumb at all.

Celebrity abductions of the specific type that Gavin Plumb was alleged to have been planning were exceptionally rare. Plenty of celebrities have experienced nutty stalkers breaking into their properties and a number of celebrities have even been murdered by crazed fans. * However, an abduction like the one Plumb was supposed to be arranging was largely (if not completely) unheard of. The singer Duffy said she was drugged, abducted and raped (the identity of her abductor remains a mystery) and the American actress Jessica Biel was kidnapped from the set of a television show when she was fifteen - though thankfully found only hours later unharmed.

In 2002, nine people were arrested in relation to a plot to kidnap Victoria Beckham and demand a $5 million ransom. This last case was obviously different from the Gavin Plumb case because it was financially motivated. Plumb's plan was sexually motivated. Celebrity abduction cases like these were very rare though. Gavin Plumb's dark if crackpot plan (or collection of plans if you prefer - it was hard to decipher a coherent single plan in Plumb's online ramblings) to abduct Holly Willoughby was pretty much unprecedented.

Gavin Plumb argued that having a celebrity crush was perfectly commonplace and is something that most people have. Plumb told the police he was not alone in having a crush on Holly Willoughby or sexual fantasies about her because she was an attractive woman and a public figure. This was not much of a defence and had no relevance to the case. Just because you like a specific celebrity that doesn't give you carte blanche to go on the internet and ask if anyone wants to help you abduct and rape them. Plumb did not have a 'celebrity crush' on Willoughby. He had a dark and deeply weird sexual obsession with her which had taken over his life.

Gavin Plumb's main defence was that thinking or posting about doing something is not the same as actually doing it. Just because he'd shared sexual fantasies about Willoughby online it didn't mean he was actually going to kidnap her to act on them. This was the general gist of his defence. The case was a lot more complex and disturbing than that though and Plumb knew it. He wanted the case to be simplistic but it wasn't. There were a number of things which made Plumb's claim that this was just a fantasy difficult to accept. There was his talk of murder, sending off for things like metal cable ties, and - most salient of all - his criminal record proving he had tried to do similar things for real in the past. It is rather difficult to claim that a man who once tried to try up two teenagers at knifepoint is no threat to anyone in the real world.

Holly Willoughby made her return to television a few months later to host ITV's Dancing on Ice. While she had been shaken by the experience (it is said she didn't leave her house for several weeks after being told about the abduction plot by the police), the fact that Gavin Plumb was now in prison at least gave her some peace of mind. Plumb himself stewed in prison while he waited for the trial. His confidence, incredulity even at being arrested for things he had said online in a private group, must have given way by now to fear and trepidation. It was obvious to Plumb that the authorities were taking his past online communications in deadly serious fashion.

The only consolation to Gavin Plumb at this time was the fact he was no stranger to prison. This was his third spell behind bars. He certainly must have been beginning to fear though the possibility that this might be a longer stint than before if the trial did not go well for him. Plumb was not being charged with saying rude or nasty things about a celebrity online. He was being charged with intent to kidnap and murder. And it wasn't a case of proving that Plumb would have really attempted to go through with this abduction plan but more a case of the defence having to prove that he WOULDN'T have gone through with it.

The salient problem for Plumb and his defence is that the

prosecution already had evidence that he WAS capable of madness like this in real life. There were four women out there who all had a similar tale to tell about how they had been threatened by Plumb - two of whom he attempted to abduct and two of whom he was in the process of restraining with tape. There were five if you counted his former partner Laura Roberts and six if you counted the woman who accused him of rape. If he didn't have these past convictions and accusations, if his slate was clean, Gavin Plumb's defence team would have had a better chance of portraying him as a sad online fantasist who would never dream of doing anything like this in the real world.

In the real world, Holly Willoughby wouldn't have touched Gavin Plumb with a barge poll. He would have been unlikely to ever meet her - not unless he got an autograph at some public event like a film premiere. That would have been it though. In the novel The Collector the theme of class is apparent throughout. Frederick Clegg is clearly from a more humble background than the bohemian, better educated and posher Miranda Grey. Clegg seems to think he can somehow bridge and cancel out this class divide by taking ownership of Miranda. There is a theory that Plumb's obsession with Holly Willoughby betrayed similar themes - even if Plumb was unaware of his own alleged subtext. Holly Willoughby went to a nice school and then made a good living from her looks when she was younger - which set her on the path to a television career and millionaire status. These were all things that Gavin Plumb could only dream of. Plumb's frightening obsession with Holly Willoughby was obviously sexual but maybe there was little tiny bit of celebrity and class envy in there too.

In his computer files the police found one in which Plumb imagined a fictional affair between himself Holly Willoughby. An illicit (and unlikely) whirlwind affair between a famous television presenter and an unemployed security guard and convicted sex pest. At some point this imaginary fictional affair then morphed into Holly Willoughby as his prisoner kept locked up in an abandoned stable. Plumb didn't leave it at that though. The fantasy refused to go away. He went on and on about abducting Holly Willoughby online. He went on and on about raping her. He talked about killing her. He purchased chloroform - or at least what he thought was chloroform. He bought a 'restraint kit' and metal cable ties. He solicited help from others online. If this was merely a fantasy it was a remarkably elaborate and vivid one. Though his crimes never actually occurred in the real world this time, Gavin Plumb's latest brush with the law was by far his most serious yet. He knew more than anyone that there was a vast electronic library of terrible threatening things he had said about Holly Willoughby and what he planned to do to her. It was going to take a remarkable barrister to convince a jury that none of this was real.

* The music icon John Lennon was killed at the age of 40 by a disturbed fan named Mark Chapman. Chapman was a security guard with mental health issues. He had contemplated suicide and become obsessed with John Lennon. He thought Lennon was a hypocrite for singing songs about money not being important despite being a millionaire who lived a lavish lifestyle. Chapman bought a gun and flew to New York where Lennon lived with Yoko Ono. He staked out the Dakota Apartments building where Lennon resided and would often sign autographs outside as he came and went from the building. Chapman even got Lennon's autograph himself before he returned to kill the music icon. Chapman later said that Lennon had been very nice and polite when he signed the autograph. That didn't stop him from shooting John Lennon dead though.

Rebecca Schaeffer was a 21 year-old actress in 1989 and starring in the CBS sitcom My Sister Sam. Schaeffer was up for a part in The Godfather III and had appeared in Woody Allen's

Radio Days. She seemed destined to use her sitcom fame as a springboard to a movie career. Schaeffer resided in the Fairfax District of Los Angeles and had an apartment in a Mock Tudor house. One day, Schaeffer heard her doorbell and rushed down thinking it was a script she was expecting to be delivered that day. Instead she found a young man outside the house who turned out to be a fan who had tracked her down. She signed an autograph for him and then he left.

Later in the afternoon, the young man returned and rang Schaeffer's bell again. This time, Rebecca Schaeffer was more short with him. She told the young man that he was wasting her precious time with these interruptions and that he should leave her alone. At this, the young man produced a gun and shot Schaeffer in the chest. She was taken to hospital but dead within an hour. The young-man who had killed Rebecca Schaeffer was 19 year-old Robert John Bardo. Bardo had become obsessed with Schaeffer and once even tried to get onto the set of My Sister Sam. Bardo's motivation for the murder was his anger that Schaeffer had done a love scene in the film Scenes from the Class Struggle in Beverly Hills

Bardo went back to his home in Tuscon after the murder but was swiftly arrested by the police. One of Bardo's sisters knew that her brother suffered from mental illness and was obsessed with Rebecca Schaeffer. When she heard that Schaeffer had been murdered she immediately suspected her brother and called the police.

Bardo was found guilty of first degree murder and sentenced to life imprisonment without the possibility of parole. The most chilling thing about this awful case was the ease with which Bardo managed to find out where Schaeffer lived. Bardo had hired a private investigator and the investigator simply found Schaeffer's address through the California Department of Motor Vehicles. The tragic death of Rebecca Schaeffer triggered new anti-stalking laws. As a result of Rebecca's murder, Congress passed the Driver's

Privacy Protection Act (which prohibits state Departments of Motor Vehicles from revealing the home addresses of state residents). The damage had already been done though. The murder of Rebecca Schaeffer remains one of the most chilling examples of celebrity 'stalking' ever recorded in Hollywood.

CHAPTER SEVEN

Gavin Plumb's trial began at Chelmsford Crown Court on Monday, June 24, 2024. This was where Jeremy Bamber was convicted. The serial killer Peter Tobin had also been in this court. Holly Willoughby waived her right to anonymity for the trial. She signed this document on the 19th of June. It read - 'I am automatically entitled to anonymity as the victim of a sexual offence. These provisions mean that no matter likely to lead members of the public to identify me as the person whom Gavin Plumb is alleged to have planned to rape... shall, during my lifetime, be included in any publication. I am also aware that the defendant is charged with two other offences where I am the victim and that automatic anonymity does not apply to those offences. My name has been widely reported in connection with this defendant and the allegations against him meaning that my ability to preserve any meaningful anonymity in relation to the alleged sexual offence has been significantly undermined. I have considered the position with care and I have decided not to seek to preserve my anonymity as the victim of the alleged sexual offences.'

The Honourable Mr Justice Murray was the judge who presided. The trial was surprisingly brief and when boiled right down to its core came down to two conflicting viewpoints. The defence argued that this was all sick online bluster by a sad lonely man and Gavin Plumb never had any intention of abducting Holly Willoughby. It was just a fantasy. The prosecution argued that it much more than online bluster and Gavin Plumb, if not stopped, would have tried to abduct Holly Willoughby for real. That was basically it. Was the defendant a sad bedroom fantasist with a vile imagination or was he really going to try and do what he spoke of endlessly online? If he hadn't been arrested would have gone through with this crazy abduction plan? Five men and nine women were sworn in as part of the jury. The public gallery was full and many reporters were in attendance.

The court clerk read the indictment to the jury before the trial commenced. She said - "Count 1: Soliciting murder, contrary to section 4 of the Offences Against the Person Act 1861. Gavin Plumb between the 2nd day of October 2023 and the 5th day of October 2023 solicited, encouraged, persuaded, endeavoured to persuade or proposed to another to murder Holly Willoughby. "Count 2: Encouraging or assisting the commission of and offence believing it would be committed, contrary to section 45 of the Serious Crime Act 2007. Gavin Plumb between the 27th day of December 2021 and the 5th day of October 2023 did an act, namely assembled a restraint kit, and formulated a plan with a third party to travel to the UK and to the home of Holly Willoughby, break-in to her home, stupefy and tie her up and by force deprive her of her liberty without her consent, which was capable of encouraging or assisting the commission of an offence, namely kidnap, believing that the offence would be committed and that his act would encourage or assist in its commission

"Count 3: Encouraging or assisting the commission of and offence believing it would be committed, contrary to section 45 of the Serious Crime Act 2007. Gavin Plumb between the 27th day of December 2021 and the 5th day of October 2023 did an act, namely formulated a plan with a third party to have sex with Holly Willoughby without her consent, which was capable of encouraging or assisting the commission of an offence, namely rape, which was capable of encouraging or assisting the commission of an offence, namely, believing that the offence would be committed and that his act would encourage or assist in its commission." Gavin Plumb wore jogging bottoms and a t-shirt when he shuffled into court. Gavin Plumb's defence barrister was the highly experienced Sasha Wass KC. Wass had successfully defended Sun executive editor Dan Wootton in the Libel case brought on by Johnny Depp.

Ms Wass certainly had her work cut out in court though because Plumb was not a sympathetic figure (to put it mildly) and the details of his online activities and conversations were beyond grim and deeply unpleasant. Plumb was also a two-time convicted sex offender - a fact which proved to be a persistent and predictable handicap to Ms Wass throughout the trial. The defence case was that Plumb's abduction plan was just a fantasy. A sick one but a fantasy nonetheless. One which was never destined to happen. The prosecution could simply remind the court though of Plumb's convictions for attempted kidnap in the past. This fact was like an anchor which kept rearing its head and dragging the defence case underwater. Plumb's past criminal convictions were a frequent thorn in the side of Ms Wass in this trial. Though the odds were stacked heavily against her client, Ms Wass put forth a valiant effort and did just about as well as anyone could have in the circumstances.

What made the task of Ms Wass especially difficult was that she had to be open about the fact that her client was a horrible person who had done (and said) vile things. Sasha Wass KC wanted the jury to forget about all of this though and just focus on the lack of plausibility in Plumb's abduction plan. This was the core strategy taken by the defence team. The trouble is though that it was impossible for the jury to forget about Plumb's past convictions when they kept being reminded of them by the prosecution. Just about the only thing Ms Wass could do was point out that Gavin Plumb's last conviction was many years ago - which indicated (the defence suggested) he had changed and didn't do that sort of thing anymore. Ms Wass suggested that this dark part of Plumb had, regrettably and distastefully, surfaced online but was no longer active in the real world.

Ms Wass argued the abduction plan was so ridiculous and far-fetched that it would be absurd to act as if it was a tangible thing which Plumb ever intended to put into operation. Ms Wass was under no illusions about the sleazy character of her client but she insisted he was not a murderous serial kidnapper who had the ability to magically make celebrities vanish or assemble teams of professional criminals for SAS style raids. The defence made great play of the fact that Plumb was very unfit and not terribly bright. They portrayed him as the last man on Earth who would actually be capable of some elaborate and taxing kidnap plan involving a big celebrity. Ms Wass was more or less telling the court that her client might have a vivid and sick imagination in online chatrooms but don't get carried away. He's not some Essex version of Ted Bundy. "His defence was made clear from the moment police entered his house in order to arrest him," said Ms Wass. "He didn't know why on earth the police had come to arrest him. As far as he was concerned, he had done nothing wrong." This was certainly true enough - to a point. Plumb was genuinely bewildered at first when his door was smashed in by the police.

In the opposite corner to Ms Wass was Alison Morgan KC. Ms Morgan previously acted as Junior Counsel for the Prosecution in the trial of those accused of murdering Stephen Lawrence. She was highly experienced and had even been involved in high profile terrorist trials. Setting out the case for the prosecution, Alison Morgan KC told the court - "The prosecution's case is that the online discussions that this defendant had revealed his real intention to carry out a plot to kidnap Holly Willoughby from her family home, to take her to a location where she would be raped repeatedly, before the defendant then intended to kill her. It's not just the ramblings of a fantasist. This defendant had carefully planned what he would do and how he would do it, purchasing items that would assist him in carrying out that attack."

Ms Morgan told the court that Plumb had said to the undercover American police officer online that 'fantasy wasn't enough anymore' and he wanted the 'real' thing. The prosecution barrister also told the court that Plumb had purchased 400 metal cable ties online. What would a man in a small flat need with 400 metal cable ties? "The offences alleged against the defendant are about the planning of the attack on Holly Willoughby," said Ms Morgan. "They are charges that focus on the defendant's attempts to solicit or encourage another to commit the offences of murder, kidnap and rape. Because the defendant's planning was interrupted, he never got to the point of actually attacking Ms Willoughby. He did not get to her address with the equipment that he had purchased to carry out the attack. That is why all of the offences are framed in terms of soliciting, encouraging and planning. The defendant's messages sought to encourage someone else to commit these offences with him. Encouragement of that type is, in itself, a criminal offence."

Alison Morgan KC said that Plumb's electronic history also displayed a sexual obsession with other celebrities and some of his neighbours. He had so many pictures of women it was impossible for the police to look at all of them. That would have taken forever. This all paled though in comparison to his Holly Willoughby obsession. Ms Morgan wasted no chance to talk about Plumb's previous offences. The defence team had tried - for obvious reasons - to prevent Plumb's criminal history from being mentioned at the trial because they argued it was not relevant to the case in hand. This was a somewhat desperate blocking operation which didn't work in the end. Plumb's past convictions were very relevant to the trial because they contradicted the main line of Plumb's defence - the claim that he was an online fantasist incapable of doing these things in the real world.

This 'victory' by the prosecution before the trial had even begun left Sasha Wass KC rather like a snooker player who now needed a couple of snookers before the frame had even started. Ms Morgan also noted that in his online discussions with 'Marc', Plumb had shared Holly Willoughby's address. "If you consider it's a fantasy of two blokes disgustingly getting off on this on a chat, why is it necessary for them to be sharing her address?" Ms Morgan said that, in his online conversations, Plumb had boasted several times about being in prison twice - as if it was some great proud accomplishment worth boasting about. Plumb had also, more than once in his online conversations, lamented the fact that his past crimes were poorly planned. Ms Morgan was obviously suggesting that Plumb had learned from his 'mistakes' and therefore put much more thought and time into his planned abduction of Holly Willoughby.

"Your task is not to assess what you consider to be the likely impact of this offending on Holly Willoughby," Ms Morgan told the jury. "The defendant's planning of these offences was interrupted by his arrest. He never got to the point of encountering Holly Willoughby. She did not meet him and the offences that the prosecution alleges against this defendant, which if carried out would have involved catastrophic violence against her, were disrupted. Your task is to determine whether those offences are established by the evidence, which comes primarily from what the defendant said in messages to others, along with what was found at his home address."

Ms Morgan told the court that the research, planning, and detail of Plumb's obsession made it go way beyond mere fantasy. If this was merely a fantasy why was he not satisfied with simply discussing Holly Willoughby online? Why all the research into her home and elaborate never-ending posts about his abduction plan? Why did he purchase his 'abduction' kit items and do research on imitation firearms and abandoned buildings? Why did he send off for a flick knife? Why did he send off for metal cable ties and chloroform? Why did he install CCTV in his flat if it wasn't in preparation for having to 'stash' Holly Willoughby there? A man living in a small council flat was hardly likely to be much of a prime target for burglars. Why was Gavin Plumb actually spending money on all of this stuff If this was simply a fantasy? One of the appealing things about fantasies and daydreams is that they don't cost you any money. Gavin Plumb on the other hand was backing his fantasy with money from his own pocket.

"If it is suggested in this trial that this was nothing more than a fantasy, discussed online with others," Ms Morgan told the court, "you will want to think about the following: the details of the planning; the persistence of the defendant; the extent to which he had researched his victim and the way in which the attack would be perpetrated; the items that he had purchased in order to carry out a real attack, all of which would have been completely unnecessary if this had been just fantasy." The court heard that Plumb had even spoken to others online on going on a tour of the This Morning studio to get 'close' to Holly Willoughby. If there was a weakness in the prosecution case it was probably the fact that Plumb never actually went anywhere near Holly Willoughby. He never visited the area where she lived or the This Morning studio. The prosecution argued though that these things were ambitions of Plumb.

In the Abduct Lovers group, Plumb said one of his ambitions was to work with Willoughby as part of her 'security'. Plumb seemed to think that a few weeks working as a security guard in an Essex business park meant he was now qualified to work as a bodyguard for one of the most famous women in Britain. Not that Holly Willoughby even had a team of bodyguards - she was a daytime television presenter not Taylor Swift. Plumb's grasp on reality never seemed to be very strong and this was something which the defence team would have to somehow try and work to their advantage. Gavin Plumb was fairly attentive in court although he did have a habit of staring at the floor when the grim volleys of his vile chat group ramblings were aired. Plumb did not have much of a moral compass and it is doubtful he was capable of genuine remorse or shame but even he was embarrassed and uncomfortable when his online words were read aloud for everyone to hear.

The second day of the trial heard from Detective Constable William Belsham of Essex Police. He talked about what was found on the defendant's electronic devices and how they'd had to get access to Gavin Plumb's phone from his legal representative because Plumb initially refused to give them his pin code. It was only on the 7th of November 2023, just over a month after Plumb's arrest, that the police were finally granted the pin code for his phone. When the police began trawling through all the material on Plumb's phone they quickly saw why he hadn't been in a tremendous rush to hand it over. The court heard the grim details of some of the messages Plumb had posted concerning Holly Willoughby in these awful chat groups when he was chatting night and day with 'Marc'.

Plumb and Mulligan talked about 'breaking her teeth', pulling her hair out, raping her repeatedly, keeping her shackled in some abandoned stable, and burning her house down. 'She has no idea what is coming on the horizon,' Plumb had messaged Marc. The court also heard voice messages Plumb had left too where he talked about the abduction. His tone, for the most part, was unemotional and matter of fact. The way he discussed these horrible thoughts and alleged plans in such a mundane way was chilling. Though he failed to actually enlist anyone in his plans, Plumb did display manipulative qualities in the chat groups. He was able to quickly impose himself on these groups and become the dominant personality among the members. Plumb kept the abduction plan going for months on the forums. He was still obsessing over the plan when he was arrested. At no time did he ever lose interest in Holly Willoughby or move onto talking about anything else.

The prosecution argued that this was evidence that he would have gone ahead with the abduction sooner or later. This bizarre and frightening obsession with abducting Holly Willoughby, the prosecution argued, hadn't gone away and never would go away until Plumb's desires had driven him to attempt something drastic for real. In a few (but only a few) of the voice messages, Plumb sounded a bit drunk. Strangely though the defence never really latched onto this. It might have been a tactic to claim that Plumb was drunk or addled when he posted or said a lot of this stuff (even if it would hardly have excused the vile nature of his messages and online conversations) though the patently sober and clear headed Plumb of most of the voice messages would obviously have made this a difficult line to maintain - which probably explains why the defence didn't bother.

Plumb was in a deep hole and an effective defence for him was not easy at all. It was very difficult. All the defence could really do was hammer home their theme that this abduction plan was stupid and plainly not supposed to be real. Detective Constable Belsham shared a number of further details from conversations Plumb had with others online. The person Plumb had talked to the most was 'Marc' (Mark Mulligan). More evidence concerning the conversations this duo had shared online merely continued the unavoidably grim aura of the trial. The court heard that 'Marc' had told Plumb in their private messaging that he had recently 'stalked' an Irish radio producer but decided not to through with an attack or abduction. The men in this group liked to mention any real life sex crime activities they'd got up to because this gave them more credibility in the group and showed they were not just online talkers.

Tragic, horrible and sad as it was, these men liked to boast about doing terrible things to impress others in the group. Plumb himself, as we have noted, mentioned his own criminal convictions more than one in online conversations as a way to bolster his status as a man who had 'experience' of the things the group spoke of. The online messages showed that 'Marc', though he often pretended otherwise, was clearly reluctant to travel to England to help Plumb and a salient factor was not just that he knew Plumb's abduction scheme was preposterously unrealistic but also because he had a criminal record. Mark Mulligan was well aware that if he had his collar felt lurking around in Holly Willoughby's garden the police were quickly going to learn of his criminal record in Ireland and he'd then be in very big trouble.

Marc told Plumb that although an English prison would probably be 'nicer' than an Irish one he wasn't entirely convinced he wanted to end up in any prison be it in England or Ireland. Marc made vague promises to Plumb that he would come to England to help but the messages tended to indicate that he enjoyed the fantasy and the 'fan fiction' of abducting a celebrity much more than the actual prospect of helping an overweight man scale Holly Willoughby's wall like some scene in a comedy film and then inevitably end up in a court and prison again soon afterwards. He therefore steadfastly remained in Dublin to dress up as He-Man and contemplate crimes against people a lot more local to him.

The court heard how Gavin Plumb had googled 'killers from Harlow' as if there was some local website where you could hire a local hitman or professional kidnappers as easily as you might ring up for a plumber to fix a leaky tap. Maybe he was just curious to see if his home town had ever produced a famous serial killer (which it hadn't). It was also revealed that Plumb had sent private messages to Holly Willoughby's Twitter account informing Holly there were deep fake nude pictures of her on the web. He of course got no reply from the admin staff running her account and the information he divulged was not exactly a secret or something they were unaware of.

Deep fake nudes on the net are something that celebrities (sadly) can't do much about even if they want to. They can't go around deleting millions of internet pages. Plumb was probably divorced enough from reality to imagine that Holly Willoughby read all her private messages on Twitter and then personally responded to them all. Perhaps he was expecting or hoping for a private message or email from Holly thanking him for this information. He probably pictured Willoughby sitting in her pyjamas at home taking great care to draft her grateful and heartfelt response to him. Holly Willoughby had seven million followers on Twitter/X. Plumb's private message was completely pointless but it did betray his desire to find some way to have contact with Willoughby.

Detective Constable Belsham told the court of a strange online conversation between Gavin Plumb and a young woman who had supposedly run away from home. Plumb told 'Marc' he had arranged to meet this woman and was planning to sexually assault her in his flat. Detective Constable Belsham said this meeting did not actually take place though and the police investigation could find no evidence that this young woman was even a real person. The presumption is presumably that the 'young woman' was a fictional creation of someone online either as a prank or for their own gratification. People on the net are not always who they claim to be and Plumb had learned this the hard way when it transpired that he been talking about his abduction plans with a police officer.

Plumb liked to think of himself as tech savvy and

streetwise but he plainly wasn't in reality. He had posted awful things on groups that were not even encrypted and he had left an incriminating trail of not just online chat but voice messages and even video messages. Plumb seemed to be unaware that police forces sometimes monitored online groups of the type he frequented. He didn't seem to realise that what he been doing was highly risky and might come back to haunt him in the future. He was so caught up in the addictive thrill of posting in these groups and allowing his darkest thoughts to roam free that he never considered the possibility that this was criminal behaviour and his abduction plans might be taken at their word.

Detective Constable Belsham would later tell the court, in response to questions by the defence, that the police never found any CCTV evidence which showed that Plumb had visited Holly Willoughby's home or street. There was no evidence that Plumb had ever taken a real photograph of Willoughby or ever visited the places where she worked or might be making a personal appearance. Plumb's abduction plan never actually got beyond his flat and computer in the end and the defence were understandably keen to remind the jury of this fact as often as they could. The prosecution argued that Gavin Plumb dearly wanted the plan to move beyond his computer more than anything in the world and was doing his level best to make that happen.

In his first court appearances in 2023, Plumb had a rather sinister goatee beard but he was somewhat more clean shaven for the trial. The defence wanted him to look as non-threatening and normal as possible. It was no easy task though because there was always something slightly off about Gavin Plumb. He was just one of those people who gave you an uneasy feeling. Plumb didn't show much emotion during the trial but he did seem to wince slightly a few times when the disgusting messages he had done through Abduct Lovers were read out. It was excruciating for him to have to sit there in a court full of people as the things he had said about Holly Willoughby were read aloud.

The American police officer who had triggered this trial in the first place by reporting Plumb to the authorities on both sides of the Atlantic, gave his evidence in remote fashion with his identity protected. "This was about identifying if this was fantasy for Mr Plumb or not, and he answered several times that it was not," he told the court. "He continued to provide me with details that make me believe he is a credible threat. When taken in the totality of the circumstances I believe this to be a credible plan and this would have been carried out with or without my services." The police officer said that in all the time he had been doing this online work he had never known anyone to purchase chloroform - as Plumb did. The police officer said that you don't purchase chloroform if you aren't serious about abducting someone. Why else would you be sending off for this stuff? "This is the first time I have encountered this matter in which a subject has purchased a chemical to render a victim unconscious," said the officer.

The defence strategy on this specific point was to argue that Plumb had bought the chloroform merely to 'show off' to his grubby online friends. He just wanted to show them a picture of it sitting in his kitchen because he knew they'd be really impressed. Sasha Wass KC, who was defending Plumb, asked the American police officer how credible the abduction plan really was. Did he really think Plumb was capable of this daring abduction - one that would require stealth, speed, criminal connections, physical fitness, and even ingenuity? Were these all not qualities and things that the shambling figure of Gavin Plumb patently lacked or hadn't acquired? The police officer replied by saying that this was a 'subjective' question.

Ms Wass reminded the police officer that Gavin Plumb was not exactly light on his feet or an Olympic athlete. How on earth was this huge lumbering clumsy man supposed to be an active participant in some daring abduction mission? "Well there is no kind way of putting this," said Ms Wass, "he was enormous wasn't he? His size and girth affected his mobility to an extent. It was difficult for him to move. He could move but he, it was difficult – he didn't have a spring in his step." The police officer conceded that Gavin Plumb was not the most spry of men and didn't have a 'spring in his step' but disagreed with defence portrayal of the defendant as someone who could barely move at the time his arrest. "He could walk fine from the video I've seen," the police officer told Ms Wass.

Ms Wass asked the police officer about Plumb's private online comments to him about dumping Holly Willoughby's body in a lake. She asked the police officer if he had then established where the nearest lake to Gavin Plumb was in order to test the credibility of this claim? The police officer said he hadn't. To the surprise of just about no one, a man from the Owatonna Police Department in Minnesota didn't have the foggiest about the preponderance of lakes near Harlow in Essex. Should he have checked this out? Possibly but it didn't seem half as important as Ms Wass appeared to be making out. Ms Wass asked the police officer if he now wished to reconsider his evaluation of how serious Plumb had really been about the abduction? The police officer said he did not wish to reconsider his analysis. His opinion hadn't changed at all. He was convinced that Gavin Plumb had posed a genuine danger to Holly Willoughby. Nothing had changed his mind about that since the arrest.

Ms Wass did, in what you could describe as a small victory, manage to get the police officer to agree that the handcuffs Gavin Plumb had sent him a picture of were not real law enforcement handcuffs by any stretch of the imagination. The handcuffs actually had a furry collar around them. They were basically novelty sex toy handcuffs and not the genuine article. Ms Wass had a bit of success with this point because she could basically say, yes, Gavin Plumb sent off for some stuff but some of it wasn't REAL stuff. It wouldn't have been much use in a real abduction. The obvious weakness with the handcuff argument by the defence was that Plumb had also sent off for metal cable ties.

* You can see then how difficult it was for Ms Wass. Each time she tried to move her pieces up the board she was quickly checked by the prosecution.

Ms Wass also asked the police officer if the fact that Gavin Plumb couldn't drive and didn't have a licence or a vehicle had not made him suspect the abduction plan was just a fantasy and not realistic. "No," replied the police officer, "it did not because in the United States it is not uncommon for someone without a driver's licence to operate a motor vehicle. I did not think it posed a problem." Ms Wass asked the police officer about Plumb's plan to steal Holly Willoughby's car after the kidnapping to use as an escape vehicle. "Was this credible at all or complete nonsense?" she asked. "It is important to evaluate if this is fantasy or not and I asked him several times and he said it was not," replied the police officer.

The police officer had been doing this online work for three years now. He said he was experienced at this task and knew the difference between an online fantasist and a genuine danger to society. In his considered view, Gavin Plumb fell into the latter category and not just the former. Alison Morgan KC, in her questions to the police officer for the prosecution, mostly took the chance to remind the court of Plumb's past convictions for crimes against women. This was a logical and effective strategy. Plumb's past sex crime convictions were a handicap the defence team always struggled to get around. The biggest weakness in their case, the fatal flaw, was always Gavin Plumb's criminal history.

* Photographs of items found in Plumb's flat by the police did reveal though that he more than one pair of handcuffs. In the video Plumb shot for the Abduct Lovers group to show

'David Nelson', he explicitly mentions that he has two pairs of handcuffs. Whether any of the handcuffs were 'legit' was not made clear but the presence of metal cable ties probably made it a moot point anyway. The items also included a whip and buckles, belts, ankle-cuffs, rope, and restraints. Plumb got some of these items from sex toy websites. One can see in the video he shot on his phone that Gavin Plumb clearly loves laying this stuff all out on the bed and admiring it.

CHAPTER EIGHT

There were fresh revelations about Gavin Plumb at the trial. It was revealed that late in 2008 he had been accused of rape by a woman who said he forced her to the floor and covered her mouth with his hand. She said the man who did this was wearing a Liverpool football top. Plumb was a big Liverpool fan and owned a replica shirt at the time. Gavin Plumb was not charged by the police - though the rape allegation was reported to them. Given what we know about Gavin Plumb now, that rape allegation should have resulted in a thorough investigation and criminal charges. Another thing we learned at the trial was that Plumb had done a number of web searches on 'Jewish women raped during the war' and 'Holocaust rape'. He had also read articles about a 2015 case where someone attempted to kidnap an air-stewardess. Plumb's other google searches included ones on 'Snapchat killers'.

When he was called to give evidence, Gavin Plumb told the judge he would be unable to stand for prolonged periods due to his weight and health so he was permitted to sit down as he spoke. Gavin Plumb had a surprisingly high voice for such a big man. He sounded a bit like the snooker player Ronnie O'Sullivan when he finally spoke. Plumb displayed reasonable intelligence in court in that his attention span did not seem to waver too much. He sat forward at times and listened carefully to everything that was said during the trial. Quite often he would fold his arms as he took in everything going on around him. Plumb insisted that what he was being charged with was not real but basically just a dark form of fan fiction. It was 'online fantasy chat' and bore no relation to reality. "It was kind of like gratification," said Plumb. "It was something I knew was never going to happen. It was a rush of excitement as I knew it was online chat to get my gratification and move on. I knew it was never going to be anything more than a fantasy."

Gavin Plumb was quite calm as he spoke. He seemed to think he had a reasonable chance of talking his way out of this tricky situation. "Chatting online and chatting in real life are two different things," said Plumb. Plumb depicted himself as flabbergasted that his online fantasies about Holly Willoughby had landed him in court on kidnap and murder charges. He insisted that he bore no malice towards Holly Willoughby and never in a million years would have harmed her or tried to attack or abduct her in real life. Plumb said he had never met Holly Willoughby nor made any attempt to meet her. Despite his online 'banter' he said he would never dream of going to her house or trying to find her in real life. Plumb said the allegation that he was planning to murder Holly Willoughby was ridiculous.

Plumb basically tried to depict this case as a celebrity crush that had got a bit out of hand online. He conceded that he had been weak and stupid in becoming addicted to these unsavoury chat groups and had posted some very regrettable and horrible things about Holly Willoughby as a consequence. Gavin Plumb said it was ludicrous though that anyone believed he was really going to carry out some twisted fantasy that he'd been stupid enough to share online. Plumb said he deeply regretted becoming involved in the sites where these sorts of fantasies were shared and it was a big mistake to have posted on them. He told the court he was embarrassed to have to hear his dark fantasies being aired in court as if they were real things that he planned to take part in.

"I completely regret this chat and I'm disgusted this has all come out," Plumb told the court after Ms Morgan asked if he wished to offer an apology for his online posts about Holly Willoughby. "I'm sorry for the contents of the chat, absolutely. I'm absolutely heartbroken, disgusted and shocked that it has come out." Plumb said that he didn't usually go in for this sort of online chat 'thing' but after befriending 'Marc' in the group his 'chats' had become darker than he'd anticipated. That was what you might describe as something of an understatement. The prosecution had a logical rebuttal in the trial in that they could simply ask why, if this was all just a fantasy that Plumb had no intention of carrying out, couldn't it just stay in Plumb's head? Why did he have to talk about it endlessly online? Why did he try to recruit people? Why did he purchase metal tie cables and chloroform? If this was truly just a fantasy then, the prosecution argued, none of this planning and purchasing of items would have been necessary.

Plumb tried vaguely to counter this but he had a difficult task. He said many people had a curiosity about their favourite celebrities and sometimes looked up their house online to see where they lived and what their private life was like. While this was probably true it was also true that most people don't share violent online abduction rape fantasies about their favourite celebrity and purchase restraints and chloroform. This contradiction was a circle that the defence never managed to square. There seemed to be a gulf between what Plumb was telling the court and the actual facts of the case. The jury were most likely picking this up already. Plumb's past criminal history and strange and disturbing internet conduct and shopping in the previous few years (all the dark online rape and kidnap talk, purchasing alarming items like restraints etc) made it very difficult to easily dismiss him as a harmless daydreamer.

Gavin Plumb's insistence that he wasn't planning to do any of this stuff in reality was though aided by his poor physical condition. This was a man who looked like he could barely tie his own shoelaces - let alone stage and take part in a complex kidnap of a major celebrity. Plumb told the court it was ridiculous to think he could have hopped over the giant wall at Holly Willoughby's house. He said he would have been more likely to trip up on a step outside and knock himself out or something. Gavin Plumb, due to the gastric band surgery, was lighter now than he had been at the time of his arrest and yet he was still incapable of standing up for prolonged periods in court. This did tend to suggest that he would have been incapable of playing much of a role in a real abduction. He'd have been out of breath even getting up a few stairs.

Plumb did not drive (a few lessons, as we have mentioned, was the extent of his driving skills) or have a car so how he was supposed to kidnap Holly Willoughby was puzzling to say the least. His plan of stealing Holly Willoughby's car sounded very unrealistic. First of all he would have to find the keys and then a man who couldn't drive would have to speed off in a stolen vehicle (which he'd be completely unfamiliar with) in South West London. There was never any evidence that Plumb had recruited a 'getaway driver' for this plan either. Much of the abduction plan made no sense sense and this was the whole tenor of the defence team in court. They argued that just because Plumb liked talking about this abduction plan online it didn't mean he was stupid enough to actually attempt it.

The defence argued that Plumb was aware that fantasy and reality are not the same thing. He was well aware that what he was saying online was fiction. His words were not meant to be taken literally. It was a logical line for the defence to take but whether the jury was buying any of this was certainly doubtful. There was a nine foot wall around most of Holly Willoughby's house. It was hard to imagine the lumbering Gavin Plumb getting over this barrier even with a ladder. Breaking into a normal house is difficult enough but this was a hundred times more difficult. Holly Willoughby did not live in a rural isolated bungalow and leave the back door open at night for the cat to come and go when she went to bed. This was a millionaire celebrity in a swanky CCTV festooned part of London in a big house with alarm systems, secure locks, secure windows, and security cameras.

Even if Gavin Plumb had gone ahead with his kidnap plan the chances of it being successfully carried out and him escaping from the scene with Holly Willoughby in tow were just about zero you'd imagine. That's the trouble with people who only live in the world of fantasy. They don't seem to realise that fantasy and reality are not the same thing. This was the crux of the trial. Did the defendant know this was a fantasy or did he think it was possible? Plumb made kidnapping Holly Willoughby sound easy in the grubby secret chatrooms he frequented. 'Bang, job done,' Plumb would say to his online friends after boasting to his online friends that Willoughby would be his captive in a matter of minutes once they arrived at her house. In the real world though kidnapping Holly Willoughby would not have been easy at all - even with the aid of a lunatic or two from the murky sewers of the dark web. The chances are they wouldn't even have managed to get inside Willoughby's house let alone kidnap her.

And what if Willoughby and her husband heard noises outside and alerted the police? How was Gavin Plumb supposed to escape from the vicinity successfully and then secretly trek all the way back to his Essex flat? Plumb tried to use these unrealistic components of the plan to his advantage in court. He conceded it might have sounded a bit like a plan in his online communications but argued that it was no plan at all when scrutinised. The not so hidden subtext of Plumb and the defence was the black humour inherent in the inadequacies of the abduction plan. They portrayed it as a laughable proposition. Gavin Plumb had said online that once inside Holly Willoughby's house, Willoughby and her husband would be restrained and he would then pause to pick out some of her outfits to take with them. It was details like this which made the plan seem more like a fantasy than something that could actually happen. Plumb clearly liked that mental picture an awful lot. To imagine himself in Holly Willoughby's bedroom going through her clothes (and doubtless her underwear drawers too).

The fact Holly Willoughby had three children was something that did occasionally factor in Plumb's discussions about the abduction but not as much as you might expect. In his online posts, Plumb said these children could be used as 'leverage' to make sure Willoughby did as she was told. Most of the time though in his online discussions, Plumb seemed to either ignore or completely forget that Holly Willoughby had three children in the house. The children were like an annoying extra detail or complication to Plumb that he preferred not to dwell on. In much the same way, he didn't talk all that much about Holly Willoughby's husband. There is an obvious theory that the jealous Plumb hated the thought of his beloved Holly Willoughby having a husband and a family. He didn't like thinking about this.

The fanciful nature of the abduction plan was then a salient part of the defence calculations and strategy. It was their best hope and the only available strategic legal life raft they could cling to. They sought to persuade the court that Plumb knew this plan was ludicrous and bound to fail. That's why he never would have actually tried to do it in the first place. He had no desire to do this for real. He liked to talk about it online and fantasise about it but that was it. It wasn't something he was actually going to do because he knew he wouldn't be capable of carrying it out.

The prosecution had an obvious counter to this line of defence though. They simply pointed out that Plumb was never planning to stage this abduction alone. They argued that Plumb always saw himself more as the organiser of this plan - not the solo participant. The prosecution had firm ground too for this line of reasoning because there was ample evidence of Plumb seeking to recruit others in the Abduct Lovers group. In fact, as we have noted, Plumb was so persistent in trying to find people to help him in the chat group that he actually started to get on everyone's nerves in the end. Many members of the group came to dread checking their inbox - lest there should be yet another private message from 'BigBear' going on and on about abducting Holly Willoughby.

Plumb told the court that the incidents where he'd tried to abduct two women on the Stansted Express were not planned much in advance and he only wrote the threatening notes (which he handed to the women on the train to make them do as he said) the night before the incidents. As evidence for this claim that he'd only done these things to get arrested and escape from his toxic relationship with Laura Roberts, Plumb said he hadn't fled the scene at all after the first incident and after he got off the train had waited patiently on the station platform for thirty minutes in the expectation that the police would arrive to arrest him. He said they never did though and so eventually he just wandered off and went home. After the second incident, Plumb said he again (rather than flee) waited around on the station platform for the police to arrest him and this time some Transport Police did arrive to take him into custody.

Gavin Plumb's claim that he had done all of this merely to escape from Laura Roberts contradicted the established facts in that at the time he was still living with Laura and they were together for a while yet. If life was so unbearable at home why were they not separated? On what planet is abducting women on a train the only way to escape from an unhappy relationship? Asked in court where he had acquired the fake gun and rope for these failed train abductions, Plumb replied (rather dubiously) that he had found them on the grass in a park - which completely contradicted what he'd told the police at the time about the imitation gun being left in the coat by his brother.

Alison Morgan KC said Plumb had explained at the time that the abduction attempts were a 'prank' because he was bored. Once again Plumb's evidence was bizarre and weird and stupid. If one is bored you could perhaps read a book or go for a walk. Abducting women on a train is not what you would call a traditional or conventional antidote to boredom. Ms Morgan asked Plumb if he had deliberately lied to the police in 2007. Plumb denied that he had lied to the police about the train incidents. Gavin Plumb's evidence - both in the past and present - did not stack up. It was not consistent. He had either lied to the police or was lying to the court - or both. Ms Morgan had success in these exchanges because she was making Plumb seem shifty and inconsistent. After a reasonably confident start in court, Plumb was now beginning to struggle and become noticeably frazzled.

Alison Morgan KC asked Plumb how he had felt when he approached the women he'd threatened on the train. Plumb said he felt frightened and claimed this is because he was acting out of character. Ms Morgan responded by asking Plumb how he thought the women on the train must have felt when he sat down next to them, handed them a threatening note, and then touched their leg? Plumb conceded to Ms Morgan that the two victims must have been very 'scared' but denied that he had set out to 'terrify' the women. Once again, Plumb's words did not chime with his actual actions. Ms Morgan laid bare the jarring contradiction between Plumb's words in court and his actual deeds and conduct.

Ms Morgan asked Plumb what his 'endgame' had been with the airline stewardesses and the two teenage girls in Woolworths. If he had successfully isolated and restrained them, what next? What was he planning to do to them? "Nothing," replied Plumb. This was obviously not a terribly convincing answer. Ms Morgan said Plumb had referred to the airline stewardesses on the train as 'sluts' and 'slags' in his online conversations with Marc. "Are the airline stewardesses sluts?" she asked Gavin Plumb. "I don't know," said Plumb meekly. Ms Morgan reminded Plumb he had sent a picture of an airline stewardess to Marc online and said "Tt was sluts like this who got me done." Plumb tried to shrug this off in court. He said it was just online chat and didn't mean anything.

This was a damaging session of the trial for Gavin Plumb. The last thing the defence (already fighting a rear-guard action) needed was the prosecution raking over Plumb's criminal history. In reference to the Woolworths attack on fellow employees, Ms Morgan said - "Two sixteen-year-old girls you left screaming and crying. Do you disgust yourself when you think about this?" Plumb nodded. He agreed it was disgusting. "What did it feel like when you put the tape round the wrist of that girl?" asked Ms Morgan. Plumb replied that he had been scared. "You were scared? Did you look at her face? Was she scared?" demanded Ms Morgan. Plumb weakly responded by repeating again that he was disgusted by his behaviour. Ms Morgan told the court more about the things Gavin Plumb and 'Marc' had said about Holly Willoughby. The way they had talked about knocking her teeth out, restraining her in bondage equipment, raping her, and so on. Plumb gave his familiar stock answer by replying that it was just dark online talk which he deeply regretted and nothing like that was going to happen in real life.

Plumb was at pains in court to insist that Holly Willoughby was never in any danger from him in real life and the abduction was merely an online fantasy that both he and others got involved in. Plumb's attempt in court to paint himself as a placid and reasonable sort of chap was not really working due to the avalanche of grim evidence the prosecution was throwing back him. The Stansted Express, Woolworths, Abduct Lovers. The person that Ms Morgan was (accurately) describing sounded like someone who should be prison. The trial was slipping away from Gavin Plumb at a rapid rate of knots. Gavin Plumb said that due to various factors like his weight and periods of unemployment, there were times when 99% of his life was spent online. He was looking for friends and got sucked down this rabbit hole of Holly Willoughby groups and celebrity chat groups where members shared fantasies. Plumb said he regretted the things he had said in these groups and insisted once again he wasn't like that in real life.

What obviously didn't help Plumb in court was his previous convictions against women. They didn't suggest a man who was happy to just stay in the realm of fantasy when it came to his dark desires. The defence that this was all in Plumb's head and he was harmless in the real world therefore did not wash. A man who is harmless and lives purely in his own twisted imagination and in the 'pretend' online world does not go around with fake guns threatening air-stewardesses. He does not threaten two teenage girls with a knife. The defendant had clearly been on the ropes when Ms Morgan had grilled him about his convictions. Plumb said he had not intended to cause his victims any distress - which was patently a preposterous statement. You don't threaten a sixteen year-old girl with a knife and start trying to tie her up and not cause distress. You don't sit down next to a woman on a train, put your hand on her leg, and tell her to get off at the next stop with you without causing terror and distress.

The prosecution wasted no chance to bring up Plumb's past convictions during the trial - which was a shrewd and obvious tactic. Even if one was inclined to think the Holly Willoughby kidnap allegation was absurd on the face of it, Gavin Plumb's grim past made you stop and think. He was capable of awful things when it came to his treatment of women and had the criminal slate to prove it. Plumb's claim that his past crimes were done because he wanted to get arrested and escape from his relationship with Laura Roberts was also not very convincing. Why not just leave Laura Roberts if life with her was so terrible? It was very bizarre and patently ridiculous to claim that the only way out of a toxic relationship is to try and abduct some women on a train. Plumb's defence team must have winced at these moments in court where the defendant dropped one of these ludicrous explanations and undid any modest progress that Ms Wass might have been making on his behalf.

Ms Morgan asked Plumb why he had done so many general web searches about rape and then so many posts in the Abduct Lovers group about rape. Why was he so obsessed with rape? Did he find it exciting? In response, Gavin Plumb said he was researching rape at the time to help a friend who was raped in real life. He said decided to research the subject so he could be more understanding and helpful to his friend. Gavin Plumb did himself few favours with answers like this. If one were genuinely researching the subject and crime of rape to be more understanding and comforting to a friend who had suffered one herself would you really be typing 'Holocaust rape' into your search engine as Plumb was proven to have done? Ms Morgan then told the court that Plumb had done web searches on the rape of a four year child and then sent details of this to his friend Marc online. Why had Plumb done this? The flummoxed and embarrassed Plumb could supply no logical answer as to why he had done this. The real answer was obvious and disturbing. He had done these searches because he found them exciting.

Plumb was taking a forensic battering from Ms Morgan and

painfully struggling to find any vaguely logical or believable answers for the questions she was asking. During the trial, Gavin Plumb actually tried to portray 'Marc' (Mark Mulligan) as the person who led him astray online. Plumb said that Marc's 'chats' were darker than he expected and he sometimes responded with one word answers just to get rid of him online. None of this chimed with the digital evidence - which indicated Plumb was every bit as bad as Mulligan and actually the dominant figure in this twisted cyber friendship. Alison Morgan KC told the court that Plumb had talked online about how he was waiting for an accomplice to book time off work so that the abduction plan could go into effect. She told the jury that if this was all in Plumb's head and something he wasn't planning to do why was he impatiently talking about waiting for his accomplice to become available?

It seemed unlikely though that this person, whoever it was, was truly planning to help Plumb. The members of the chat group were not exactly reliable. Most of them seemed to be aware that fantasies are not necessarily things that will happen in the real world. The prosecutor Alison Morgan KC sought to cast doubt in court on whether Gavin Plumb was really as immobile as he made out. She argued that around the time of his arrest he had been fit enough to get work as a security guard. Ms Morgan argued that Plumb was exaggerating when he claimed to be largely inert and housebound circa the last months of his freedom.

At the time of his arrest, Plumb has lost a decent amount of weight. By the time of the trial he had lost more weight still. He was still heavy by most standards but he was (thanks to the gastric band surgery) just over ten stones lighter than he had been at his absolute heaviest. At the time of the trial, Plumb was fitter and more mobile than he had been for years. The defence were at pains to remind the court that though, when the alleged kidnap plan was nearing some sort of final decision, Plumb was heavier than the man sitting in court.

The prosecution (as one would expect) took a different approach. They argued that Plumb was not, contrary to how Plumb and the defence might spin this, some housebound man who could barely walk when he was arrested. The prosecution agreed he probably couldn't have carried out the abduction alone but he could have played some sort of leading role with other people helping.

The prosecution further argued that Plumb's weight loss (thanks to a diet and surgery) had been motivated by his desire to be fit enough to take part in the Holly Willoughby abduction plot he had cooked up. The prosecution showed the jury the police video of Plumb's arrest in court to show that he was mobile and able to walk around his flat at the time of his arrest. The debates over Plumb's weight got a trifle confusing in the end if truth be told because Plumb's weight did fluctuate a lot - only downwards of late rather than up. The prosecution were right to point out though that Gavin Plumb seemed fairly mobile in the video the police released of his arrest at his flat. He was standing up and walking around. At this time he was in employment and went to work each day so he must have been reasonably fit if he was able to do that. There was no question he was ambulatory and in better shape than he had been for years.

Around the time he did the interview for the BBC about obesity back in 2018, Gavin Plumb truly was inert and housebound. That was no longer the case in 2023. Where the defence did have some traction though was in pointing out that Gavin Plumb, even with the gastric band aided weight loss, was still not Daley Thompson. It was rather difficult to picture him vaulting over Holly Willoughby's wall and creeping around her house and garden like a ninja. The fact that Plumb was in employment at the time of his arrest did indicate though that Plumb was in pretty good health all things considered and perfectly able to get out of the house. In a sense then the debate over his weight and fitness was something of a score draw between the defence and prosecution. The defence were able to put forth a reasonable argument that the lumbering Plumb would have been inept in an abduction whereas the prosecution suggested he wasn't quite as lumbering and inept as he made out.

Contrary to the digital evidence that had been accrued from the chat groups, Gavin Plumb denied in court that he'd done any extensive research on Holly Willoughby's house and security. He claimed in court he hadn't the faintest idea of what her security was or if she drove herself to work. Plumb said he had once shared a picture of Willoughby's house online but he found that on Google Earth. Once again though he was not terribly convincing when he said this in court and it did tend to clash with the digital evidence from the Abduct Lovers group - where topics like Holly Willoughby's house and security had patently been of great interest to Plumb. It was a bit rich for him to now claim that these things had never concerned him and he was completely clueless when it came to them.

Plumb, under questioning by the defence, told the court he was never serious about the abduction. It was all 'bravado' purely to impress the online group he was part of and the friends he had made there. Asked if he thought at the time that 'David Nelson' (the American police officer) was really serious about taking part in the abduction, Plumb replied by saying that he didn't know. Plumb said he was suspicious of Nelson in the end because the airline ticket he supplied evidence of buying seemed to have a new name on it - not the name Nelson had supplied in private messaging. The odd thing was that while 'David Nelson' asked Plumb as many questions as he could without attracting suspicion, Plumb did not reciprocate in the same fashion. These people he spoke to online mostly remained quite fuzzy to Plumb. He never asked them too many detailed questions or went out of his way to find out more about them.

Gavin Plumb told the court that he didn't drive and didn't have the faintest idea how to get to Holly Willoughby's house by public transport. He said he would have no clue which train or bus to take to get from his home in Essex to South West London. This was not terribly credible because in online messaging he had offered to give 'Marc' detailed directions to get from London airports to to his Essex flat - should Marc decide to pay him a visit. Plumb clearly knew a lot more about London transport links and routes than he was willing to let on in court. There was even online evidence too that Plumb had actually worked out the route from his flat to Holly Willoughby's house. Plumb said he never believed his online 'friend' Marc was really going to help him in the abduction plot/fantasy. "In the conversation I felt like we were building some kind of friendship. I never expected him to come to the UK, I thought it would be someone I would chat online with. I never expected him to come, I never expected him to say that he's coming or whatever."

For the defence, Ms Wass, rather shrewdly, told the court that in order for the alleged abduction to be successful, Gavin Plumb would have needed to get inside Holly Willoughby's house. This would have required Plumb forcibly breaking in because it was rather unlikely that the Willoughby family left their front door unlocked and the windows open at night when they went to sleep. So the defence (already knowing full well what the answer would be) asked Gavin Plumb if he had any experience of picking locks and breaking into houses. Gavin Plumb said he wouldn't even know where to start and had never picked a lock or broken into a house in his life.

Thanks to lifestyle magazines and Instagram we know that Holly Willoughby's gigantic and lavish front door has stained glass windows and elaborate gold handles. It's safe to say you wouldn't be rushing down the bookmakers to put too much money on Gavin Plumb picking the lock on this door or breaking it down. What didn't help Plumb in court was that the police had evidence he had conducted specific online web searches in relation to where Holly Willoughby lived. This contradicted his verbal evidence that he didn't know much about where she lived and wouldn't know how to get there. In one of his online chats with Marc, Plumb had talked about a railway bridge and alley near Willoughby's house. Plumb clearly knew a lot more about the house and location than he claimed in court.

Alison Morgan KC had an effective tactic for the prosecution in the way she reminded the jury of the more mundane details of Plumb's abduction plan. Her point was that endlessly talking about the logistics of the plan online wasn't 'sexy' and not exactly exciting fantasy talk. Ms Morgan argued that Plumb's obsession with these mundane details meant the abduction was credible and real. "What's sexy or gratifying about boring details?" Ms Morgan said to the jury. She argued that there would be no need for the 'boring' details of Plumb's plan if it was merely a fantasy confined to the internet. Ms Morgan also argued - not for the first time - that Plumb's extensive planning for this abduction was a consequence of the fact that he got caught the last two times and didn't want to repeat that mistake.

Ms Morgan told the court that Plumb had also done extensive web searches on abandoned buildings in which one might secretly hold a person captive without anyone knowing. Plumb had said online more than once that he had found an abandoned stud farm which would make the perfect place to hide a captive celebrity. The 'abduction kit' that Plumb purchased and put together consisted of metal cable ties, handcuffs x 2, ankle-cuffs, a ball gag, a whip or 'flogger', and a blindfold. The police and prosecution alleged that Plumb had acquired this stuff to use on Holly Willoughby. Plumb denied this allegation. He said it was BDSM package he had purchased online in the hope of 'spicing' up his love life with a former lover. It is probably fair to say that Plumb's claim was considered somewhat dubious on this front though whether he really planned to use this 'kit' on Holly Willoughby was another question altogether.

The prosecution asked Plumb to name the ex-lover on whom he planned to use this BDSM kit with but Plumb said he refused to name a name because he said it wouldn't be fair on that person. His inability to name this alleged 'ex-lover' was obviously not great for his defence because it made it look like this person didn't exist and Plumb had just made it up. In all probability that was exactly what he had done. Just made it up. It was another one of those strange moments in the trial where Plumb suddenly turned into a little boy who was claiming that the dog had eaten his homework. Alison Morgan KC described Gavin Plumb as 'sly' and a 'liar' in court. It was hard to disagree with those statements. If this trial was a boxing match, right now Gavin Plumb was behind on points and rapidly running out of rounds in which to overturn the deficit.

CHAPTER NINE

Gavin Plumb's defence team told the court that his online fantasies about Holly Willoughby were simply the 'ravings' of a lonely man about a celebrity he knew he would never meet in real life. What didn't help though was the violent and explicit nature of these 'ravings' - so violent and explicit in fact that the press were not allowed to report the full details of them. Sasha Wass KC, defending Plumb, told the court that while his posts and comments in relation to Holly Willoughby were vile and misogynistic he never had any intention of visiting the celebrity's house in real life and the kidnap plot was simply a grubby fantasy that he had been foolish enough to speak of online as an escape from his mundane and often disappointing life. Ms Wass agreed that what Plumb said online was deeply unpleasant and unacceptable but said it did not mean any of this was real. Gavin Plumb, insisted the defence once again, was not really going to abduct and murder Holly Willoughby.

Although the online chat group that Plumb had posted a lot of this stuff in was private it wasn't exactly military level security. There was a weird blind spot with men like Plumb in the way they thought they could say whatever they wanted online with no ramifications. It didn't seem to occur to them that places like Abduct Lovers attract the attention of police online crime prevention teams. The vastness of the internet and the millions of pages, websites, chat groups, and forums make it difficult for police forces though. The police are like little spaceships investigating the endless cosmos one star at a time. Plumb clearly thought Abduct Lovers was a secure place where his posts and messages were only being read by people like his online friend Marc. He turned out to be completely wrong about that.

Men like Plumb seemed to think this is what the internet had been invented for. To cater to the grim 'ravings' of misogynists and sex offenders. All of that information and entertainment on offer and they chose to congregate in a chat room discussing which celebrities they'd like to abduct and rape. This is where they chose to spend their free time. It spoke volumes about their true character. Sasha Wass KC argued that Plumb's previous convictions should not be held against him because he was very young at the time, had pleaded guilty, and these things happened a long time ago. He had not done anything like this for many years so this, the defence suggested, proved he had changed - at least as far as the real world and real crimes were concerned. Yes, his conduct online required some sort of sanction or warning (or therapy even one might venture) but strictly in relation to this case, the Holly Willoughby case, Plumb had not done anything wrong. He had not gone anywhere near

Willoughby's house and he certainly wasn't really going to murder her.

This was the general gist of the defence. Ms Wass asked the jury to consider only the case now under trial. Plumb's past convictions, Ms Wass argued, were not relevant to the matter in hand. The only thing the jury should concern themselves with, argued Ms Wass, was the plausibility of Plumb's alleged plan to abduct Holly Willoughby. Was this abduction plan at all realistic? Did he really intend to go through with it? Was it not simply sick bluster from a lonely man trying to impress people online and channel some of his dark desires into the online world where they would harm no one? This was the general line that Ms Wass took in court. She had to plant seeds of doubt in the minds of the jury and the most obvious way to do that was brush Plumb's past convictions under the carpet and point out how ludicrous his alleged abduction plan was when looked at in the cold light of day.

It was a strangely odd sort of trial given the gravity of the proceedings and the copious media interest. It involved no murders. There was no forensic evidence. There were no eyewitnesses called to give evidence - simply a couple of police officers. The defendant had never met the victim. The crime had not even been committed when the defendant was captured. The crime was never in fact committed at all - though this of course is the whole point of good police work, to stop crimes before they take place! The other odd thing about this trial was how short it was. In the era of Lucy Letby we are sort of accustomed to trials going on forever. Gavin Plumb's trial by comparison to most was very short.

The trial hinged on the evidence given by the American undercover police officer and the disgusting digital spew Gavin Plumb had left on the internet. The jury had to decide if this spew of threats and plans had genuine intent beyond cyberspace. It was what you might describe as a trial of the modern age. In the past dodgy and dangerous characters like

Gavin Plumb would be isolated but hiding in plain sight. These days they had their own internet chat groups to hang around in and use to talk to fellow sex offenders. Gavin Plumb did reasonably well at times during the trial but he couldn't keep this going on a consistent basis. Once the prosecution got their teeth into him he quickly started to unravel and it became apparent that his evidence was all over the place.

Plumb had his best period early on in the trial when he managed to convey a sense of bemused disbelief that everyone was acting as if he'd done something for real when in reality he had merely said it on the internet. Where he didn't do so well though was when he was pressed on something by Ms Morgan and then suddenly pulled out some ridiculous whopper of a lie that no one believed. Gavin Plumb was a not a very convincing liar and the defendant's chair in a courtroom trial is literally the last place that an unconvincing liar like this wants to be. There was almost a childlike quality to some of Plumb's lies. Some of them were positively eye-rolling.

Alison Morgan KC reminded the court that Plumb had initially shown great reluctance to give the police his phone pin code. This, Ms Morgan argued, was plainly the action of someone with quite a lot to hide. When she asked Gavin Plumb in court why he had been so reluctant to give them his phone pin, Plumb replied that he was reluctant because he didn't trust the police. When asked why he didn't trust the police he refused to be drawn too much on the issue - aside from suggesting it was something to do with his ex-partner Laura Roberts. This presumably was a reference to the time he been arrested for domestic violence and suspicion of rape.

Plumb had over 10,000 pictures of Holly Willoughby in an electronic folder called 'Holly'. These were mostly normal photographs taken from the web and ones which anyone could find through an image search. He also allegedly had 86 AI videos of Holly Willoughby on his phone. These odd AI videos had a fake version of the celebrity which could be made to talk. The police said though that they could not access this 'AI Holly Willoughby' that Plumb was supposed to derive great amusement from. Plumb also had a collection of fake doctored images where Holly Willoughby's head was put on the body of a woman in a pornographic pose or scene. In some of these images the women were tied up. There were literally millions of images of celebrities and women on Plumb's devices so it was impossible for the police to trawl through all of them. He was evidently not someone who deleted stuff or cleared out his folders very often.

One thing which definitely didn't help the defence team was that Plumb had some chloroform in his flat that he'd purchased from a homeopathy website. If he wasn't planning to kidnap anyone why did he have two bottles of chloroform? Plumb, rather unconvincingly, told the court he had purchased the chloroform to clean up a stain on his carpet and clean the fridge. Chloroform is a colourless, sweet-smelling organic compound that was historically used as an anaesthetic. It is a volatile liquid that can induce sleep and unconsciousness when inhaled or ingested in large amounts. However, due to its harmful effects on the liver, kidneys, and central nervous system, chloroform is no longer commonly used as an anaesthetic. Chloroform is assuredly not something you'd want to be using to clean your house or fridge. Plumb was well aware of that. His desperate lie was, well, desperate.

The two bottles of chloroform that Plumb had purchased were later opened by the police. When the police lab tested them they found that they contained ethanol (a flammable toxic liquid) and water. Junior prosecution counsel Rosalind Earis told the court - "The bottles purporting to be chloroform found in Gavin Plumb's bedroom were tested in a laboratory and found to contain ethanol and water. No chloroform was detected. The laboratory analyst noted that homeopathic liquids are typically prepared by the extreme dilution of the purported active ingredient using water and/or ethanol, to the point where none of the active ingredient is detectable in tests." What this confusing statement basically meant was that the homeopathy website had either swindled Plumb or used a process to try and hide the chloroform. If the former it was certainly an interesting business decision by someone. Pretending to sell chloroform but not actually selling chloroform. The website pocketed money without actually supplying any potential lunatic with real chloroform.

When he had been asked by the police after his arrest he why'd sent off for chloroform, Plumb had simply responded by saying it wasn't illegal to own chloroform. That wasn't a very good answer and his explanation for having chloroform in court was even worse. The prosecutor Alison Morgan KC told the court that Plumb had done a number of web searches on how long chloroform takes to knock a person out. Ms Morgan also noted that Plumb had not done a single solitary web search on the cleaning qualities of chloroform or how to get stains off the carpet. Plumb's explanation for owning chloroform was therefore quickly exposed by Ms Morgan as complete nonsense and another obvious whopper of a lie. "Not Vanish, not any other product on the market," Ms Morgan told the court. "Not 'how good is chloroform at getting a terrible stain off my carpet?'" The defence tried their best to counter this by showing the jury a carpet stain in Plumb's flat which they said had refused to go away through conventional means.

Alison Morgan KC, in her closing statement, told the jury that Gavin Plumb would almost certainly have carried out his abduction plan if 'David Nelson' had turned out to be a real person who was willing to help. Ms Morgan said that considerable planning went into Plumb's scheme and he was a grave danger not just to Holly Willoughby but to society. A man with all these dangerous thoughts and plans, not to mention criminal convictions for attempted kidnap offences, couldn't possibly be given the benefit of the doubt. The prosecution wanted a life sentence. Gavin plumb must have feared the worst by now. Despite how unrealistic the abduction plan had been he certainly had not won any hearts and minds in the court - especially when they heard about his past convictions and the awful things he had said online. Plumb had plainly struggled under the precise questioning of Ms Morgan. She had made him look shifty and untrustworthy. Ms Morgan had unmasked the real Gavin Plumb. He WAS shifty and dodgy. This was not a man you'd trust - especially when it came to women.

Ms Morgan said this case had been devastating and 'life changing' for Holly Willoughby and although Willoughby had supplied a victim statement it would not be read out at this time (the prosecution did though read a victim statement from a previous victim of Gavin Plumb). Ms Morgan told the jury that the defence claimed Plumb's words were simply words and not something he was actually going to do. She pointed out though that when 'David Nelson' gave Plumb proof of an airline ticket and said he was coming over to help in the abduction plan, Plumb did not do an about turn and tell him not to come over and say it was just a fantasy. On the contrary, Plumb seemed happy and excited at the news that David Nelson was apparently on the way across the Atlantic Ocean to Essex. This, the prosecution argued, is because Gavin Plumb had finally got what he wanted and what he had searched for so desperately - help in his planned abduction of Holly Willoughby. A willing accomplice.

"When he believed that 'David Nelson' had just booked a flight to travel from the US," said Ms Morgan, "to join in that attack - [he said] 'it's really happening'. He didn't say 'don't do that, I was just kidding'. He didn't say 'this is just fantasy, you haven't bought a flight have you?' He didn't say 'I don't really trust you because the name on your flight booking doesn't match with your username'. After years of planning he had finally found someone who didn't appear to have cold feet." Alison Morgan KC told the jury that the argument Plumb lived only in fantasy groups online and wouldn't do these things in real life was not true because his past convictions showed he had already crossed the threshold into reality when it came to his dark desires. The prosecution argued that the 'it is only a fantasy' argument was impossible to apply to Gavin Plumb because we knew from his criminal history that he was capable of doing these things for real.

"He has terrified, subdued, threatened and detained real women against their will," said Ms Morgan. "He has carried weapons for that purpose. He has carried ropes for that purpose. Real people exist in the world now who were threatened and touched by this man and he was looking to learn how to avoid those mistakes again; looking to make sure that he didn't fall into the errors that led to women being able to get away from him." Ms Morgan told the court that Gavin Plumb was not to be trusted and had told a tissue of lies throughout this case. "I suggest to you that he is a prolific liar and that he's tried to minimise the extent of his criminality to you, and if you agree with that, what does that tell you when he stands there and tells you it's all just fantasy?"

Ms Morgan said there was a 'nasty reality' to Plumb - which was a clever phrase given the trial essentially hinged on fantasy versus reality. Gavin Plumb, said Ms Morgan, was so awful he even shocked the other members of the dreadful online chat groups he frequented. And with that the prosecution rested their case. It was going to take a Rumpole of the Bailey level speech by the defence to claw anything from this case now. In her closing speech for the defence, Sasha Wass KC said it was absurd to think that Gavin Plumb could have really jumped over Holly Willoughby's wall, broken into her house, and then driven her to his flat. Ms Wass said this was all just an elaborate fantasy that Plumb, to fill the emptiness of his life, had got sucked into. It was a horrible fantasy and he'd said some horrible things in the chat group but Gavin Plumb knew it was just a fantasy. He never visited Holly Willoughby's street or stalked her. He had no intention of abducting her in reality.

Ms Wass also told the jury that the handcuffs Plumb was allegedly going to use on Holly Willoughby were not even real handcuffs. They were cheap flimsy sex toy handcuffs that wouldn't have restrained anyone. If he was seriously going to abduct someone and keep them captive wouldn't he have got hold of real handcuffs? Ms Wass told the court that Plumb's abduction talk online was nothing more than "the ramblings of a rather sad person" and the plan was "riddled with flaws - it was wholly unachievable." Ms Wass said Plumb had stupidly and weakly allowed himself to get drawn into chat groups where "similar lonely, disaffected people were feeding off their fantasies" and egging each other on in a sort of competition over who could say the most outrageous things.

Ms Wass said that the Abduct Lovers group that Plumb had posted on, while unpleasant and distasteful, was full of sad bedroom bound fantasists and not reality. It was not a cyber den of wealthy professional kidnappers and deadly killers who were all actually going to do this stuff. Ms Wass said that the undercover police officer had even acknowledged this himself. It was only Gavin Plumb that he'd taken seriously in the group. The police officer took Gavin Plumb at his word - something which Ms Wass argued was mistaken. Ms Wass told the court that all the 'planning' Plumb had supposedly done for the abduction was simply an extension of the fantasy. None of it was something he actually planned to do in real life. She argued that Gavin Plumb was not capable of this abduction by any stretch of the imagination and he was well aware of that himself. Her point was simple. How can you convict a man of a crime he didn't do and wouldn't even have been capable of doing?

Sasha Wass KC accused the American undercover police officer of 'leading' and encouraging Plumb on the Abduct Lovers forum. It was the police officer, according to the defence, who had 'progressed' the abduction plan by constantly prompting responses from Plumb. This attention made Plumb feel important. He liked the idea that he was a 'big character' on this forum so he played to the crowd (which in this specific case was David Nelson) and said ourageous things. Plumb gave the audience on Abduct Lovers what he thought they wanted to hear. Ms Wass said Plumb had not 'solicited' the help of the police officer at all until the police officer (posting as David Nelson obviously) had begun asking him questions about Holly Willoughby. Ms Wass was arguing that Plumb, in the spirit of this dreadful place he was posting, was coming back with all of this horrible stuff in an attempt to impress Nelson. But just because it was horrible that didn't make it real. It wasn't something that happened or was ever going to happen. It was just a lonely man saying crazy horrible stuff online.

Ms Wass insisted that Plumb "had neither the means nor the opportunity to carry out any of the things he mentioned in his chats. All of the offences remained at the planning stage. He never left his house during any significant time and had never been to the area where Miss Willoughby lived. He was not able to drive, did not have access to a car and was completely incapable of scaling any of the perimeter walls of her house as he fantasied about doing during the course of his online chats. Even if he got to her house, there was no viable plan of how she would be kept at his address with the other people in adjoining flats. It is putting it highly to say it was a carefully planned operation. Many features of the plan were so unworkable that the plan could not in fact have taken place. We say it was not a sophisticated plan."

"The fun - if that is the right word - was fantasising," said Ms Wass, "the pretending that the plan would be put into effect. There is no doubt that Gavin Plumb sent the messages and there is no doubt that the content of the messages are vile and misogynistic - and Mr Plumb himself accepted they were dark." Ms Wass constantly reminded the jury that Holly Willoughby had a nine foot wall around her house. She was once again asking the jury to consider how likely it was that Gavin Plumb could get over this wall. How likely was it that he would have even attempted to get over the wall? Not very likely at all Ms Wass suggested. The subtext of the closing speech by Ms Wass was obvious. Get real, she was telling the jury, this idiot was not really going to abduct Holly Willoughby. This is stupid. Yes, he's a creep but don't bang him up for something he didn't do and something he couldn't have done.

Under the circumstances it was just about the most logical approach for the defence to take. However, Ms Wass was always fighting a losing battle in the trial. She had less to work with than the prosecution. Gavin Plumb's criminal background and absurd lies in court (purchasing chloroform to clean his carpet, buying the restraint kit for a lover he refused to name, researching 'Holocaust rape' online to help a friend who had been raped etc) were handicaps that the defence plainly struggled to work around. Sasha Wass KC had done her duty and mounted a competent defence of Gavin Plumb. All she could do now was hope that the jury agreed with the defence that Gavin Plumb's abduction was indeed absurd and never something that was destined to be put to the test. It didn't take long at all though for Ms Wass to be disappointed on this front. The jury consisted of eight women and four men. They only took just over twelve hours to decide that Plumb was guilty of soliciting murder, incitement to rape and incitement to kidnap. His guilty verdict came on the 4th of July, 2024.

Gavin Plumb did not show much emotion during the trial but he did at the verdict. For the first time he seemed emotional and on the verge of tears. Though he must have feared the worst the actual verdict still seemed to come as an unexpected shock to him. It seems that Gavin Plumb could never quite grasp the concept of someone being charged for things they had threatened online. He seemed to have the attitude that he could say whatever he wanted to online and it was no one else's business. The problem is though that if you endlessly talk about abducting and raping and even killing someone online and you have past criminal convictions for attempted abduction AND have chloroform, metal cable ties, and BDSM restraints in your house, well, the authorities have no option but to take all of this seriously.

And for all of Plumb's insistence that this just a fantasy, a jury had just decided otherwise. The BBC showed the sentencing remarks of Mr Justice Murray live but kept having to interrupt the feed when the more shocking details of the trial were read out. In his summing up the judge said he didn't think Gavin Plumb abduction plan was very realistic. It probably wouldn't have been successful. But the intent was there and Plumb's history showed that he had tried to something similar for REAL more than once. Even if it hadn't been Holly Willoughby the chances are that Plumb would have tried to abduct some poor other woman in the future because his online 'ravings' were no longer enough to put a brake on his darkest desires.

The verdict of the legal system was that Plumb should be detained to protect women. He was a pressure cooker about to blow. Plumb simply couldn't be trusted. It was somewhat ironic that Gavin Plumb, who had relished his tiny moment of fame on the BBC website in 2018, was now the main story on all the news bulletins. Fame at last but for all the wrong reasons. "This is not a case of such extreme seriousness that it is necessary to impose a whole life order," said the judge to Gavin Plumb at sentencing. "Accordingly, I must determine the minimum term that you must serve for each of these offences. If I had been sentencing you to a determinate sentence, taking account of the numerous aggravating and limited mitigating factors in this case, after a trial I would have sentenced you to concurrent sentences of 24 years' imprisonment for each offence. Because you would have served up to two-thirds of that sentence in custody, I fix the minimum term which you will serve at two-thirds of 24 years: that is, 16 years.

"Finally, I reduce that minimum term of 16 years by the number of days which you have spent on remand in custody: 280 days. This means that the minimum term which you will serve before the Parole Board may consider your possible release is one of 15 years and 85 days. It is most important that you and everyone concerned with this case should understand what this means. The minimum term is not a fixed term after which you will automatically be released but is the term that must be served before the Parole Board can undertake their first review of the case. They will review the risk that you then present and will consider whether you can properly be released from custody subject to licence at that stage and, if so, on what terms. If and when you are released, you will be subject to licence; and this will remain the case for the rest of your life. If for any reason your licence is revoked, you will be recalled to prison to continue to serve your life sentence in custody."

The short version of the long summing up was that Gavin Plumb had been sentenced to 15 years in prison. "Fifteen years to kill myself," he shouted as he was led away from the court. As he was still a relatively young man, providing he behaves himself in prison, Plumb can still probably expect to experience a number of years of freedom in the future. It will depended on many things though. He won't just waltz out of prison when the time comes. A decision will have to made over whether he is deemed fit for release. It is said that Gavin Plumb's loyal mother stood by him after the conviction. She did though, wisely, continue her custom of avoiding the media and making no public comments about the case or her son. We have no idea what Mrs Plumb made of the trial but can probably guess that she didn't think her son was really planning to abduct Holly Willoughby and was not deserving of 15 years in prison.

Mark Mulligan, the Dubliner who was revealed to have been Plumb's online friend 'Marc' and an enthusiastic participant in the twisted abduction conversations relating to Holly Willoughby, endured protests outside of his house in Clongriffin in North Dublin in the aftermath of the trial and had to have police protection. The police also took the step of seizing his computer and phone. The Gardaí (the national police service of Ireland) were informed about Mulligan's links to Plumb by the Essex Police. There were a fair few news stories about Plumb in Ireland in the wake of the Gavin Plumb trial. Mulligan actually had a past conviction in Ireland that was similar to the Plumb trial in that he had argued that things he said online were just stupid things he had said and not real. It was revealed that in this other case (not the Plumb case) Mulligan had said online - "...love to have a cottage in the middle of nowhere and take kids there and rape and torture them... and **** on their graves. Every time I heard someone got raped it's a turn on – even more when they are killed."

During that case, Mulligan had told the Irish police - "I was only saying it, I was never going to meet anybody. We were discussing fantasy rape, as far as I was concerned nothing would be done about it. It was fantasy talk only. I get obsessed talking about rape and torture, I know I need help, I wish I didn't have these thoughts. I was lonely, curious, I felt like I was an undercover reporter, trying to get information. I didn't have any real friends, I distanced myself from reality. I just wanted to talk to people." Mulligan denied that he had a sexual interest in children - despite some of his posts suggesting otherwise. After the Gavin Plumb trial gave Mulligan an unwelcome spotlight in Ireland he had to flee from his home. He now faces a fresh police investigation. Mulliogan must deeply regret getting involved in the Abduct Lovers group and becoming chatty and friendly with the user known as 'BigBear'.

Essex Police's Senior investigating officer Det Chief Insp Greg Wood said of the Gavin Plumb verdict: "Today Gavin Plumb starts a life sentence, with a minimum of 16 years behind bars, and the streets of Essex are safer for woman and girls as a result. He is a dangerous individual with a history of kidnapping, attempting to kidnap and plotting to kidnap women and girls. In this case he went further and intended to rape and murder his victim. He tried to claim throughout the trial that he was an obsessive fan and a fantasist – that is simply not true. He planned this attack on Ms Willoughby over a two-year period, scoping her movements, seeking to elicit help from others to carry out his wicked plan, buying chloroform and other items to incapacitate, restrain and inflict violence upon her.

"He is no fantasist - he's a calculated, violent, sexual predator who has spent his adult life inflicting or plotting to inflict harm on women. This case has brought violence against women and girls and misogyny to the fore. It has demonstrated that all of us, whoever we are and whatever we do, have much to do to stamp out this scourge on our society. It cannot be right that men like Gavin Plumb are able to join online forums where they vent their hatred towards women and girls and plot to harm them. In this case our American colleague ensured we were able to bring Plumb to justice, but we need everyone to stand up to call out misogyny and to report those committing or intent on committing violence towards women and girls."

Nicola Rice, a specialist prosecutor in the Crown Prosecution Service, said after the trial: "Gavin Plumb is a dangerous man who plotted unspeakable violence against one of the nation's most familiar faces. Despite his attempts to pass himself off as a harmless fantasist, the prosecution persuaded the jury that Plumb posed a very real threat. I hope his conviction brings some comfort to Holly Willoughby and her family, and shows others that the Crown Prosecution Service will always seek the strongest possible charges against those who plot violence against women." One person very happy to see Plumb convicted was his ex-partner Laura Roberts. "I am so happy, I'm over the moon to be honest," she told the Sun newspaper. "I can hardly explain how I feel. It is the biggest relief of my life. I feel safe, finally. I feel like our kids are safe with him behind bars and now he can't have any influence on them. I want to thank the judge for doing this for us and for making all women safer in this country. I hope he (Plumb) never gets out and they throw away the key. I have known for over 25 years how evil this man is. If he is on the streets, then I would also warn all women and their daughters to be careful and stay away from him. He is a predator."

Gavin Plumb's estranged father Adrian Broad spoke to the Telegraph newspaper after the trial. "It's just sick, it really is. He needs help, he definitely needs help," said Broad. "It was the [abduction] kit and what he was going to do to her, that's what disgusted me. He was little when I left. There's one thing I'm glad that his mother did, though, and that was change his surname. I don't think he's getting the support. I've seen the pictures of him and he's let himself go. I just think he's been basically dumped, especially after he's got in trouble before. I do feel sorry for him. It was a regret not just where he's ended up now, it was a regret for all of them really. What we couldn't get our heads round was how the ****- did he get a security job when he has been away, when he has been locked up? How the hell did he get that job?"

Gavin Plumb's step-brother actually did an interview after the trial but he wished to remain anonymous and did not reveal his name or face. He said of Gavin Plumb - "He was clearly one of those people where the one thing he was doing all day was watching telly. You got This Morning on from nine til one, so watching her (Holly Willoughby) for what, five hours a day? I can imagine that's where his obsession came from. In my personal opinion, I don't think prison will do a thing, because he's still got access to television and he's going to have the same obsession." Gavin Plumb's step-brother didn't seem to hold out much hope for Plumb. He didn't think he was going to change.

There was criticism after the trial of WhatsApp and Kik - which Plumb had used extensively. The Essex Police said that these companies should do more to moderate their platforms and the people who use them. There was a lot of international police frustration with these types of companies and not just in Essex because net companies were notoriously difficult to talk to and get information out of in a police case. If you had to deal with one of these companies in relation to a crime facilitated by the net you could probably expect a circuitous bureaucratic Orwellian nightmare trying to get any information or a response.

Amazingly, the Abduct Lovers chat group actually remained on Kik even after the Gavin Plumb case. A journalist for Sky news accessed the site in the summer of 2024 but said the search function on the group didn't work. The journalist was not sure if the site was now blocked or if his account was simply blocked. Sky said they reached out to Kik for a comment but - predictably - the company was not exactly forthcoming when it came to a response. It was like trying to get blood out of a stone. Police forces and justice systems are having to constantly adjust and adapt to the challenges posed by the internet. The bottom line is that if you use the net to threaten someone, incite hatred or violence, harass or bully, or talk about raping and killing someone, then you should face consequences. It is not a defence to say this is not real because it only happened online. That would not be tolerated in society so it shouldn't be tolerated on the net either.

At the start of 2024, Holly Willoughby had jetted off to Costa Rica to shoot a reality competition television series starring Bear Grylls. It was reported that Willoughby had much more stringent security these days. Despite her fame she had led a fairly ordinary life away from the camera before Gavin Plumb. This had all changed now. Her victim statement was released after the conviction. "I will forever be grateful to the undercover police officer who understood the imminent threat, and to the Metropolitan and Essex police forces for their swift response," said Willoughby. "Thank you to the Crown Prosecution Service, the Rt Hon Mr Justice Murray, Alison Morgan KC, the members of the jury and all involved in this case for ensuring that justice was done and that the defendant will not be able to harm any more women. I would also like to commend the bravery of his previous victims for speaking up at the time. Without their bravery, this conviction may not have been possible."

CHAPTER TEN

Holly Willoughby was replaced on This Morning by Cat Deeley - who was also once a children's television host and lad's mag pin-up in her younger years before graduating to mainstream presenting duties. ITV were evidently trying to replicate the same sort of formula with Holly's replacement. Deeley now hosted the show with Ben Shephard but the viewing figures plunged without Willoughby (and Phillip Schofield) so This Morning ended up as a weird victim of collateral damage in the grim and rather strange tale of Gavin Plumb. This Morning just didn't quite feel the same without Holly Willoughby. The tragic sudden deaths of a number of contributors to the show and the well publicised troubles of

Willoughby and Schofield made at least one tabloid wonder if This Morning was the victim of some Omen style curse. It wasn't of course but clickbait like this was too much of a temptation for the tabloid (and probably a fair few online browsers too).

There was some talk in the media of one of the American streaming giants approaching Holly Willoughby to do a documentary or perhaps even 'docu-drama' about the Gavin Plumb case. Willoughby has, understandably, not talked about the case though - besides a victim statement. She has got on with her life and gone back to work. In August, 2024, it was announced by ITV that Holly Willoughby would host a revamp of the quiz show You Bet! with her Dancing on Ice co-host Stephen Mulhern. Willoughby was putting the Gavin Plumb case behind her and getting on with her career.

There was obviously a lot of media attention on the Gavin Plumb case - especially once the verdict was rendered. For days after the trial there were endless stories about the 'depraved loner' who was foiled at the last minute as he set off with armed hitmen to kidnap and murder Holly Willoughby. The case was more complex than that but this was the slightly misleading surface headline way it was sometimes reported. Late in July, 2024, it was announced that Gavin Plumb was planning to appeal his sentence. It seems highly unlikely that this will be successful but he didn't have too much to lose by trying. Some of the media thought Plumb should have got a harsher sentence. They wondered why a man convicted of plotting Holly Willoughby's abduction and murder was not locked up forever and the key thrown away.

There were some contrary views too though. Some felt it was strange that Plumb had been convicted and banged up for a crime he never carried out and probably never could have carried out and yet murderers, terrorists and violent criminals frequently get more lenient sentences than Plumb or are let out of prison early. Chay Bowskill, the coal hearted and evil young man who violently abducted his estranged girlfriend, and then caused her catastrophic injuries when she fell out of the van he put her in, actually got a lighter sentence than Gavin Plumb. Was that fair? It's hard to imagine any public tears would have been shed if Chay Bowskill (who was a thief, burglar, and abusive to his former girlfriend before nearly killing her through his insane kidnapping actions) had been locked up for a longer time.

Who was worse? Plumb or Bowskill? How does one compare such awful people? The fact that Plumb was convicted not for a crime but for a crime he was planning makes the question even more complex. Would the sentence have been the same if the target of Gavin Plumb's online threats and misogyny had not been a major celebrity? Would the same police resources have been allocated to the case? What if Plumb's online abduction and rape/violence talk had revolved around not Holly Willoughby but a woman working in one of his local chip shops? It is hard not to think, in those circumstances, Plumb might have escaped with a slap on the wrist, token sentence, or a warning rather than a trial and fifteen years in prison - which is obviously not right because all women, be they Holly Willoughby or anyone else, deserve the same protection and respect from the justice system.

The counter to the view that Gavin Plumb's conviction and sentence was a little over the top was that he had tried to abduct or restrain four women in the past and got what you could describe as fairly light sentences for these crimes. He had also been accused of rape by two other women but somehow evaded any charges over these allegations. If you were to say that Plumb's fifteen year sentence for the abduction that never happened was karma or belated punishment for his past crimes then many might feel that sounded more fair. That sounded like justice. It clearly would be impossible also to completely dismiss Plumb's online 'ravings' as a harmless fantasy that never could have happened in a million years. There was plainly something deeply wrong and frightening going on in Plumb's head which warranted investigation and serious therapy.

Plumb seemed to think it was completely normal to go online for hours on end and talk about raping and killing female celebrities. That was basically his daily (and nightly) routine for a couple of years. Log into chatrooms and talk endlessly about how one might abduct and rape Holly Willoughby. Though we have no idea what experts made of Gavin Plumb in custody, he displayed signs of narcissistic personality disorder (NPD) and antisocial personality disorder (ASPD). People with NPD exhibit grandiose self-importance, a sense of entitlement, and a lack of empathy for others. Plumb's narcissistic traits fuelled his need for attention, admiration, and control.

It is likely that these traits facilitated his manipulation of others, enabling him to influence and coerce those online. ASPD, on the other hand, is characterised by a disregard for others' rights, manipulative behaviour, and a lack of remorse or guilt. Individuals with ASPD often display a pattern of deceit, impulsive behaviour, and a disregard for social norms. Plumb's antisocial traits aligned perfectly with the actions he committed. His lack of remorse for his past convictions point to the presence of ASPD. There was a lot of talk about Gavin Plumb being an 'incel' in the aftermath of this case. Incel is short for involuntary celibate. It refers to a self-identified group of individuals, primarily men, who feel unable to find romantic or sexual partners despite desiring them.

The incel 'community' often discusses feelings of frustration, loneliness, and social isolation, and it has been associated with a variety of online forums where these experiences are shared. While some individuals within this community express feelings of rejection and a desire for companionship, the term has also gained notoriety due to instances where some members have expressed hostility towards women, often blaming them for their circumstances. These negative attitudes can sometimes escalate into misogyny, and in extreme cases, some individuals have committed violence based on their beliefs.

Whether Plumb was an 'incel' or not is open to question. He was basically a sex pest and potential/actual rapist who had become frustrated that his activities in this regard were curbed by his criminal convictions and then his weight problems. This led him down the rabbit hole of vile places like the Abduct Lovers group. But fantasy probably wouldn't have been enough for Gavin Plumb in the end. His desperation and frustration in his communications with that group became increasingly apparent over time. Plumb is desperate for this stuff to be real. This was the fuel for his addiction to these groups. In his messaging on the Abduct Lovers group one can detect his frustration at not finding a serious and credible accomplice willing to assist him in real crimes. This is why he took the bait dangled by the American police officer who posted as David Nelson.

Gavin Plumb was apparently an avid true crime buff and enjoyed books, documentaries, and podcasts about real life criminals. There is actually a theory that his dark abduction fantasies might have come from reading about people like David Parker Ray, Leonard Lake and Charles Ng, and the Railway Killers. David Parker Ray was a (suspected) American killer and (verified) rapist who turned his motor home into a torture dungeon. When he was apprehended in 1999 he was dubbed The Toy-Box Killer. Parker Ray held women hostage in his soundproofed 'dungeon truck' as sex slaves. They were greeted with a terrifying audio message from Ray in which he explained how hopeless their situation now was. Parker Ray was said to have spent $100,000 turning his motor home into a torture dungeon. His motor home was like some horror film dungeon on the inside. It contained whips, chains, clamps, leg spreaders, sex toys, surgical blades, saws, and syringes. There was a gynaecologist's chair and skull-shaped electric candelabra. An FBI agent named Patty Rust had to spend days in David Parker Ray's motor home to catalogue his crimes as The Toy-Box Killer. She was so distressed by the experience she shot herself.

Leonard Lake and Charles Ng were a notorious serial killing duo who abducted, raped and tortured from 1983 to 1985. Lake was the boss of the duo and although Ng was much younger he was no less sadistic. These two evil men were both crazy. They had a military background and were into survivalist conspiracy theories. They might have killed 30 people although the verifiable figure is around eleven. They built a special bunker to keep their victims captive as sex slaves. The Railway Killers were John Francis Duffy and David Mulcahy. In the early 1980s these two men attacked young women at various railway stations in the London area. They were serial rapists and killed three of their victims. The two men would drive around and look for vulnerable women who were making their way home at night. The early rapes took place near stations in North London.

Of course, Gavin Plumb never killed anyone and we have no idea if he would have actually been capable of doing that. The true crime link is just a theory. Many of us enjoy (if that's the right word) and are fascinated by true crime but in a morbid sort of way because terrible crimes are alien to us and things we can't really comprehend. How do you make sense of a Dennis Nilsen or Jeffrey Dahmer? You can't really. We don't dream of replicating the crimes we've read about but a few troubled souls do though and perhaps Gavin Plumb was one of them. Murder was alien to Gavin Plumb but stalking and threatening women certainly wasn't alien to him. That made him different from normal people for a start.

But how bad could he have been given half a chance? What was he really capable of? Could he have graduated from bungling abductor to serious violence and murder? That's a difficult question to answer but we have enough information to say with a fair degree of confidence that he was certainly capable of rape. As for murder, Gavin Plumb has got to the age of 37 without attempting to kill a single person so it seems very unlikely that he truly harbours an insatiable urge to kill.

The question of whether Gavin Plumb would have gone ahead with an attempt to abduct Holly Willoughby is hard to say with any certainty. The jury were clearly convinced that he would have done this if not stopped but we simply don't know for sure. Plumb certainly made no attempt to visit Willoughby's home or do any 'stakeout' research. He liked to talk online about gathering first hand information about Holly Willoughby's routines but he never actually did anything like this. This was basically the foundation of his defence team's strategy in court. They portrayed Plumb as the 'pub bore' of the Abduct Lovers group. The blowhard who likes to hold court and dominate the conversation. They insisted though that Plumb was trapped in this metaphorical pub and all his talk was just hollow bluster with no shape or meaning. Plumb's planning for the abduction amounted to boasting about it endlessly online and sending off for some restraint and chemical items - much of which turned out to be shoddy and largely useless. He never actually found anyone willing to participate in the abduction - except for 'David Nelson', who turned out be an undercover police officer.

What if David Nelson had been a real person though and had flown to England to help Gavin Plumb? If this had happened would Plumb have attempted the kidnapping? Once again it is hard to say with any clear sense of certainty. Plumb's abduction plan was never very logical or planned very well. Many of the details were vague and improbable. Did he even actually find a remote safe place where Willoughby would have been held captive? He never did - despite his ramblings about an abandoned stud farm. And how long could a celebrity hostage have been secretly stashed in an abandoned stable? Essex was not the Amazon jungle. The odds of Plumb transporting Holly Willoughby to this stable would have been pretty long you imagine.

In the novel The Collector, the captive Miranda Grey writes of her abductor Frederick Clegg - 'It is me. I am his madness. For years he's been looking for something to put his madness into. And he found me.' Gavin Plumb's own madness locked onto Holly Willoughby and refused to let go. This madness only ended when he was arrested. Gavin Plumb liked the fantasy of owning Holly Willoughby as his own personal plaything. This fantasy basically took over his life for months. If ever there was a person in desperate need of a normal hobby it was Gavin Plumb. With time on his hands and nothing to do he became addicted to these sick online groups where men spewed forth their darkest desires and most hateful parts of themselves.

The question in court was whether this all consuming fantasy had tilted into reality. Was he now so desperate, so committed to this Holly Willoughby fantasy, that it was no longer a fantasy? That was the verdict of the prosecution and the jury. They believed that Plumb would have tried to do this sooner or later. Whether it would have been successful or not is another question but they believe he would have at least tried. The main problem for Gavin Plumb's defence in court was unavoidably his two convictions in the past. He approached two airline-stewardesses on a train with rope and a fake gun and clearly wanted to get them off the train as his captive. There was also the incident at Woolworths where Plumb tried to restrain two teenage girls at knifepoint. And there was Laura Roberts too - who accused Plumb of rape and domestic violence. There was also the woman who accused Plumb of raping her in 2008.

This was a total of six women who had personal evidence of just how dangerous a person Gavin Plumb truly was. These incidents were not online fantasies. They happened for real in the real world. In hindsight, Plumb should have got a harsher punishment for these past crimes. He should have been monitored more closely once he was released. He should have been banned from talking to other sex offenders online. While the question of whether Gavin Plumb really would have attempted to abduct Holly Willoughby is difficult to answer with 100% certainty it seems highly probable that Plumb's frustrations would have led him to attempt something like this with someone - even if it wasn't Holly Willoughby. A neighbour, a stranger in a park or on a train. After all, Plumb had form in this area. He had previous. He'd done this before so there was no concrete reason to believe he wouldn't do it again given half a chance - especially now that he was losing weight and becoming fitter.

For this reason the conviction and sentence of Gavin Plumb seems less harsh than it did at first glance. Society is clearly none the worse for not having Gavin Plumb walking its streets for a while. In fact, society is safer with this man behind bars. Women are safer. Gavin Plumb will up for parole one day and given his relatively young age he will most likely (health permitting) be a free man for a good few decades in the end. How different a person he is by then will depend on his rehabilitation in prison and whether age and punishment has tamed his darkness and sick desires. He will be on probation for the rest of his life.

Gavin Plumb doesn't have an awful lot to show for 37 years on this planet, at least nothing that is good, decent, or worthwhile. He will though have an enduring, strange, and dark fame thanks to the events of 2023 and 2024. His name, if it comes up in the future, will forever be linked to Holly Willoughby. He will be remembered as that sad loser who spent two years online talking about abducting, raping, and killing Willoughby and ended up (much to his surprise) in prison as a consequence. Whether he really would have done it doesn't really matter in the end. He had those thoughts and he shared them. He shared them endlessly to anyone online who would listen. He shared them so much they no longer sounded like a fantasy in the end. And he did terrible real things too to real women.

Looking at the big picture, and not just the Holly Willoughby case, one might venture that Gavin Plumb's 2024 sentence was overdue just desserts for all the awful things he has done. Plumb now has plenty of time to stew on all of this in prison. It is doubtful that he has any genuine remorse over the things he said online about Holly Willoughby or what he did to Laura Roberts, Emma and Louise, and the airline stewardesses because Gavin Plumb is not really that sort of person. When he looks back on the days when he was often unemployed and sometimes housebound due to his weight, Gavin Plumb doubtless has one big regret though as he languishes in his prison cell. He must dearly wish he'd never started watching This Morning.

REFERENCES

https://www.essexlive.news
https://www.judiciary.uk/wp-content/uploads/2024/07/R-v-Gavin-Plumb-sentencing-remarks-final-version.pdf
https://www.manchestereveningnews.co.uk
https://news.sky.com
https://www.bbc.co.uk/news

Photo Credit

https://commons.wikimedia.org/wiki/File:Holly_Willoughby.jpg

SPakhrin

26 November 2006

Other Books by Katherine Smith

Kim Edwards - The Twilight Murders

Mary Bell

Shannon Matthews

Tia Sharp

Lucy Letby - The Complete Story